Seasons with the Spirit

Seasons with the Spirit

A compilation of prayers and meditations
from *All Year Round*

Compiled and edited by Ruth Harvey

CHURCHES TOGETHER
IN BRITAIN AND IRELAND

Churches Together in Britain and Ireland
Inter-Church House
35-41 Lower Marsh
London SE1 7SA
Tel: +44 (0)20 7523 2121; Fax: +44 (0)20 7928 0010
info@ctbi.org.uk
www.ctbi.org.uk

ISBN 0 85169 267 2

Published 2002 by Churches Together in Britain and Ireland

Produced by Church House Publishing

Copyright © Churches Together in Britain and Ireland 2002

Further copies available from CTBI Publications, 31 Great Smith
Street, London SW1P 3BN Tel: +44 (0)20 7898 1300; Fax: +44
(0)20 7898 1305; orders@ctbi.org.uk; www.chbookshop.co.uk

Designed by Church House Publishing
Typeset in Optima 10/12pt
Printed by Creative Print & Design Group, Ebbw Vale, Wales

Contents

Preface	Edmund Banyard	ix
Introduction	Ruth Harvey	xi

Creation and beginnings   **1**

Be still	Ann Lewin	2
Aspiration	Jamie Wallace	3
The word awaited	Kate McIlhagga	4
Disclosure	Ann Lewin	5
Prayer of preparation	Christine Odell	6
Seven days	Bernard Thorogood	7
Morning	John Oldershaw	8
Creator God	Duncan Wilson	9
Bone of my bone	Janet Morley	10
Hanta Yo	Gwen Cashmore and Joan Puls	12
Listening in	Denis Blackledge	14
On entering church	Judith Stevens	16
Prayer of confession	David Temple	17
Prayers of adoration and confession	Vince Gilbert	18
Tingle factor	Denis Blackledge	21
So many things I can't believe	Edmund Banyard	23
Being still	Bruce D. Thompson	24
Why I never wash	Anonymous	25
Lord of life – feed me	Bruce D. Thompson	25

Advent to Epiphany   **27**

Come as a girl	Helen Wangusa	28
Come Emmanuel	Christine Jones	29
The Way	Lesley Steel	30
The call to worship	Vince Gilbert	31
Still waiting	Denis Blackledge	35
The Annunciation	Kenneth Carveley	37
Magnificat: the mystery of Mary	Kenneth Carveley	38
Angels	Ann Lewin	40
He came to his own home	Wang Weifan	41
Carol for a dark age	Rosemary Wakelin	42
Round the back in Bethlehem	Adrian Stokes	43
Incarnation	Ann Lewin	46
A child's prayer at the crib	Eva Ratcliffe	47

Contents

Christmas Communion	Michael Powell	48
Christmas	David Blanchflower	49
After Christmas	G. M. Breffitt	50
Twelfth Night	Ann Lewin	50

Lent and Passion   **51**

Ash Wednesday	Hilda Mary	52
Palm Sunday	Edmund Banyard	54
Tears	David J. Ford	56
Good Friday	Edwina Sherrington	58
Women and the cross	Simon Bailey	59
The stones cry out . . .	Ernest Smart	67
Cross-carrying Jesus:		
a prayer of confession	Kate McIlhagga	69
This is the day they		
call good	Ron Reid	70
Meditation – nails	Adrian Newman	72
Dying Stranger	David Jenkins	74
Powerful silence	Sheelah Stevens	75
Holy Saturday	David Blanchflower	76
In search of a roundtable	Chuck Lathrop	78
To women and to men	Janet Morley	80
The supper	Roddy Hamilton	82
Reflection	Ivor Smith-Cameron	85

Easter   **87**

Affirmation of faith	Roddy Hamilton	88
Resurrection	Peggy Day	90
The gardener	Margaret Crawshaw	91
Easter prayer	David Flynn	92
Bus to Emmaus	Brenda Jackson	94
This is my . . .	David M. Owen	96
Before the Easter icon	Kenneth Carveley	97
Nine seasonal collects	Suzanne Fageol	99
But nobody went		
to his burial	John Rackley	102
Become our resurrection	David Jenkins	105
A psalm of Falling		
and Rising	Allan R. Smith	106
Christ the healer	Hugh Cross	108

Pentecost and the life of the Church   **111**

A litany of thanksgiving	Kenneth Carveley	112
Who travelled to		
follow Christ's Way	Stuart Jenkins	114
A meditation on a storm	Daphne Fraser	115
Holy Spirit come	Geoffrey Ainger	117
Love, truth and openness	Alastair Dykes	118

Prayer rosary	Kate McIlhagga	120
Disciple	Godfrey Rust	121
Help us to admit our emptiness	Kate McIlhagga	122
Authority from being sufferers with Christ	Jonathan Martin	123
A Laodicean estate agent writes	Godfrey Rust	124
On the edge	Peter Brice	125
Belonging: children's meditations and prayers	Gumley House School	128
A question of language	Daphne Fraser	130
A prayer for the parish	St. James' Church NY	131
The healing of laughter	Mary Teed	132
Send your Holy Spirit	Nicola Slee	133
Thank you for your presence with us	Betty Hares	135

Harvest **137**

Heard at Harvest	Brenda Jackson	138
The dandelion	Denise Creed	139
Work is love made visible	Author unknown	140
A dancer	Weoley Castle Community Church	141
Three farmers	Morag Walder	142
Help us to be true to our calling	David Blanchflower	145
Credo from Nicaragua	Anonymous	147
Before the harvest	Edmund Banyard	148
Agriculture and rural life	Michael Powell	149
I ask for daily bread	Inazo Nitobe	151
The web of creation	Daphne Fraser	152
White powder	Michael Powell	154
The bread of life	Kathleen Allen	155

Endings and peace **157**

At the ending of the day	Kenneth Carveley	158
Contra-genesis	Anonymous	159
On the sudden loss of a child	Kenneth Carveley	161
After a still-birth	Edwina Sherrington	162
The source of peace: an intercession	Edmund Banyard	164
In time of anxiety or fear	Daphne Fraser	166
Listen	Anne Doyle	167
For mourners	Kate McIlhagga	168
Peace be with you	Hilda Mary	169
Standing on the edge	G. M. Breffitt	170

Contents

God's peace	Ikoli Harcourt Whyte	171
Blessings and benedictions	various	172
At a time of death	Michael Powell	174

Prayers for everyday life   **175**

We belong to one another	CCRJ	176
Aching void	Mary Teed	177
Mr Ordinary	Jonathan Martin	178
Technology	Michael Powell	179
Windows	Michael Powell	181
A story of God's heart	Maureen Conroy	182
Deliver me from nice people!	Daphne Fraser	186
Proverbs 31 – a meditation	Clare Sealy	187
Love	Jamie Wallace	189
The secular is sacred	Michael Powell	190
The gift of children	Christine Odell	191
A prayer for unity and peace	Society of Friends (Quakers)	192
For times of relaxation	David Blanchflower	193
Tapestry	W. S. Beattie	193
Meditation with silence	Christine Bull	194
An old person prays	Lillian Columbine	195
Out of the depths	Ann Lewin	196
Free to be	John Stuart	197
It is not uncommon to talk to God	Dennis Brutus	198
Sleepless nights	G. M. Breffitt	199
Meditation on the Lord's Prayer	Author unknown	201

Index of authors	205
Index of titles	207
Index of first lines	209
Acknowledgements	211

Preface

Within easy reach as I write are fifteen binders which contain all the material so far published in *All Year Round*.

It was in 1984 that the Standing Conference for Unity in Prayer, linked with the then British Council of Churches, began to consider how some of the often excellent prayers, meditations, dialogues, sketches, songs and hymns, written in the first instance for use in a limited situation, might be made available to a wider constituency.

Eventually, in 1987, *All Year Round* was launched offering annually to subscribers a ring binder and four packs of material, one sent each quarter. A small ecumenical editorial team was established and Dennis Duncan and I were invited to become joint editors. Dennis had to withdraw during the first year owing to pressure of other work, but *All Year Round* has survived the disappearance of both the SCUP and the BCC. With three of the original editorial team still serving, it is now published by Churches Together in Britain and Ireland.

Reading through the items which Ruth Harvey has selected for this book I am again aware of the freshness of approach so often shown, of the wide range of experience upon which we have been able to draw and how little it matters from which branch of the Christian Church the contributions have come.

I hope you will enjoy and be able to make good use of what you find here and if you do, maybe you will become a subscriber and/or a contributor to the ongoing *All Year Round*.

Edmund Banyard
June 2001

Introduction

What is prayer? Is prayer the rhythmical, private naming
of our deepest concerns and hopes, or is it a collective
thanksgiving for all that God has done? Is prayer voiced,
shouted, anguished, or is it silent and reflective? In this
collection of prayers and meditations, gathered from *All Year
Round*, it is clear that prayer is all of these things and more.
The prayers in this volume are not only a testimony to the rich
creativity of writers in Britain and Ireland and beyond, but also
to the rich spiritual life that is alive and well in these islands.

Since it began in 1987 *All Year Round* has offered a fresh
and exciting new approach to the gathering of private and
public worship material. It has been, and continues to be
a vehicle through which worshippers and worship leaders
can experiment with new ideas, and from which they can
draw inspiration.

In this volume I have brought together a selection of material
from the first ten years of *All Year Round* (1987–1997). The
selection has been put together in two ways. Firstly, I
unashamedly admit to making my own, personal, highly
subjective selection. Readers can judge for themselves whether
I have a balanced approach to prayer. Secondly, and crucially,
I canvassed the opinions of *All Year Round* subscribers, asking
a selection of subscribers to submit their ten favourite pieces.
From these two approaches, I then put together this collection.
I hope it inspires others to further creative writing, and to an
exploration of prayer which opens up the practice to the many
who already pray, and to those who do not. The date at the
end of each entry indicates which year it was included in *All
Year Round*.

The selection begins with prayers and reflections on the theme
of Creation and beginnings, ending with prayers for everyday
life. In between are prayers for use throughout the Christian
year, beginning with Advent and Epiphany, moving through
Lent and Passion, Easter, Pentecost and the Life of the Church,
Harvest, and Endings and peace. It is my hope that this pattern,

together with the indexes, will help the reader to find prayers, meditations and reflections which speak to their own particular condition, situation and need.

I would like to thank Barbara Albone for her sterling work in typing the manuscript, and Anne van Staveren and Bensela Persaud from CTBI for their support in seeing this publication through to the end. Finally, I would like to pay tribute to the Living Spirituality Network, which is committed to exploring the meaning of prayer and the search for an integrated spirituality in today's world. Without the support of the LSN Management and Reflection Groups this volume would never have been completed.

Ruth Harvey
Summer 2001

For further information about the Living Spirituality Network contact:
LSN, The Well at Willen, Newport Road, Willen, Milton Keynes MK15 9AA. Tel: 01908 200675; email: Win.Kennedy@ctbi.org.uk

If you would like to subscribe to *All Year Round* please write to Churches Together in Britain and Ireland, Inter Church House, 35-41 Lower Marsh, London SE1 7SA

Creation and beginnings

Be still

You do not have to
Look for anything, just
Look
You do not have to
Listen for specific
Sounds, just
Listen
You do not have to
Accomplish anything, just
Be.
And in the
Looking, and the
Listening and the
Being; find
Me.

Ann Lewin 1989

Aspiration

That we may learn
to listen until we understand
before replying;
to read right to the end
before reviewing;
to see all sides
before judging –

to consider the possibility
that those with whom we disagree
may be right;
that those whom we dislike
may be good;
that those whose success we envy
may deserve it.

to savour a diversity of folk
without feeling obliged to assess them;
to appreciate beauty
without wanting to possess it;
to love many people
but worship only God.

Jamie Wallace 1987

The word awaited

Sometimes,
I long to call
words of praise
to me,
so that they may settle
like doves on my palm.
I long to coax them
down from the trees
into my waiting hands.

Sometimes they come,
swift and powerful
like hawks to the wrist of the falconer,
words of challenge,
fierce words of regret.

One time You came,
The word.
Not at my call,
You came
to occupy
a cradle,
a grave,
my heart,
the universe.
You came to call me
to unleash
words of comfort
words of hope.

Sometimes
I hold out
my empty hands
and wait.

Kate McIlhagga 1994

Disclosure

Prayer is like watching for the
Kingfisher. All you can do is
Be where he is likely to appear, and
Wait.
Often, nothing much happens;
There is space, silence and
Expectancy.
No visible sign, only the
Knowledge that he's been there
And may come again.
Seeing or not seeing cease to matter,
You have been prepared.
But when you've almost stopped
Expecting it, a flash of brightness
Gives encouragement.

Ann Lewin 1989

Prayer of preparation

'Be still and know that I am God.' (Psalm 46.10)

Be
do not do
or pretend to be
anything
just be.

Be still
calm those
anxious, unruly
whirling thoughts
into stillness.

Be still and know
as the flower knows the sun's rays
as the mouth knows bread
as the heart knows love
open yourselves to knowing.

Be still and know that I am
here and now
around you and within you
behind you and before you
wherever you are
I am.

Be still and know that I am God
your Father and Mother
your Companion and Healer
your Life and your all.

Be.
Be still.
Be still and know.
Be still and know that I am.
Be still and know that I am God.

Christine Odell 1990

Seven days

Imagining
Planning
Deciding
Gathering
Shaping
Inspiring
Resting

In moment
or millennia
creation is your
world again.

How perfect is your act,
how splendid the cosmos,
how glorious the fish by the reef,
how lovely the hands of the baby,
how light is your palette of colours,
how fresh the breath of your winds.
Now let us sing Alleluia.

But what was the cry of your word?
We cannot forget the pain
in every act of creation,
that struggling to keep things right
when dreams are drowned in the mud
and life is taken on the cross.
Remake us, Lord, to sing Alleluia.

Bernard Thorogood 1993

Morning

*This piece was written as a voice-over to 'Morning' from
Grieg's Peer Gynt Suite. The . . . indicate a pause to allow
music to add to the meaning. Careful rehearsal before
presentation is advised in order that the music may
match and enhance the words.*

It is morning . . .
A shepherd sitting on a hill watches the
red glow increase . . .
and sees the pale sun creep over the
horizon. Night has gone . . .
Day is here . . . and it is very good.

At the horizon the darkness disappears,
and the distant hills, once black, now
stand against the sky . . .

The sun rises higher . . .
and, as it does so, the water of streams
and lakes reflects that light.
Dry land, and the water, may be
distinguished . . . both are calm and good.

There appear trees, then bushes, flowers
and grass . . . and, as the sun warms the
ground, birds sing, animals scuttle
home, or wake up and begin their work.
All is pleasant, calm and good.

At last, the shepherd becomes aware of
himself; sitting, looking down on the world.

A new day has arrived, and with it the
realisation that the world has a
pattern, God's pattern, and it is very
good . . .

John Oldershaw 1990

Creator God

Creator God,
taking undiluted delight
in continually throwing back
the boundaries of the universe,
a million suns declare as many dawns
whilst stars and planets
sing their complex music
across light years of space
for you to see and hear and know.

We, who like the Psalmist,
raise our eyes to the sky
and our thoughts towards eternity,
wonder what may be the significance
    of our being,
the purpose of the life in us.

If, as we believe,
you have engaged us in
your caring and creativity,
may it be clear to us that none of our actions
need be futile or fruitless.
Help us to know that within the mundane
there lies the potential for the miraculous.
Transform all our deciding and doing
with the consciousness of your purpose
    and partnership
and our imaginations
with glimpses of your sovereign glory.

Duncan Wilson 1995

Bone of my Bone

'Then the eyes of both were opened, and they knew that they were naked; and they . . . hid themselves from the presence of the Lord God.' (Genesis 3.7,8 RSV)

Loving Creator, we confess that as women
and men we have distorted your image in us.
We confess our misuse of power;
we have sought to dominate others,
and to impose our will by force or threat;
we have learned to manipulate and deceive,
and feared to confront injustice.

We repent before God, and before our sisters and brothers.

Men   You are bone of my bone.
Women   And flesh of my flesh.

We confess our misuse of our faculties:
we have prevented ourselves
from feeling compassion and tenderness;
we have failed in courage and understanding,
and denied the gifts we have.

We repent before God, and before our sisters and brothers.

Men   You are bone of my bone.
Women   And flesh of my flesh.

We confess our misuse of sexuality:
we have found pleasure in the degrading of others' bodies;
we have failed to respect and care for our own bodies;
we have chosen to condemn, rather than to delight in
    each other.

We repent before God, and before our sisters and brothers.

Men   You are bone of my bone.
Women   And flesh of my flesh.

We confess that we have failed to obey God first:
we have made an idol of our work, our status, and our
    possessions;
we have sought all our meaning in another human being;
we have made a society based on aggression and fear,
where love is a private luxury.

We repent before God, and before our sisters and brothers.

Men   You are bone of my bone.
Women   And flesh of my flesh.

We confess that we have created a world where,
between women and men, there is violence and fear,
resentment and distrust.
We seek God's forgiveness and reconciling love,
that we may learn to do justice,
and so come without shame
before the one who delights in the human race.

We affirm before God, and before our sisters and brothers.

Men   You are bone of my bone.
Women   And flesh of my flesh.

Janet Morley 1988
(*First published in* Celebrating Women)

Hanta Yo

*'Hanta Yo' is Sioux North American Indian language
and means 'Clearing the Way'*

God of surprises,
> you call us

>> from the narrowness of our traditions
>>> to new ways of being church
>> from the captivities of our culture to
>>> creative witness for justice
>> from the smallness of our horizons
>>> to the bigness of your vision

> Clear the way in us, your people,
> that we might call others to freedom and renewed faith.

Jesus, wounded healer,
> you call us

>> from preoccupation with our own histories and hurts
>>> to daily tasks of peacemaking
>> from privilege and protocol
>>> to partnership and pilgrimage
>> from isolation and insularity
>>> to inclusive community

> Clear the way in us, your people,
> that we might call others to wholeness and integrity.

Holy, transforming, Spirit,
> you call us

>> from fear to faithfulness
>> from clutter to clarity
>> from a desire to control to deeper trust
>> from the refusal to love to a readiness to risk

Clear the way in us, your people,
that we might all know the beauty and power
and danger of the gospel.

Gwen Cashmore and Joan Puls 1992
(*Ecumenical Spirituality Project of the*
Churches Together in Britain and Ireland)

Listening in

Loving Lord,
you are the one who is always there for me
as the one who listens.
You hear what I can never utter in words –
you listen to me
at a level that is too deep for words,
and you understand the sighs of my spirit.

You listen to me at those moments
when I'm not in a fit state to listen to myself.
You are there with your understanding presence
whenever I am a riddle to myself
and cannot understand my complicated
and mysterious self.
You are there when the jigsaw of my life
seems to be difficult to solve
or when pieces seem to be missing.

Your first commandment is simply – 'Listen'.
It sounds so simple, but in actual fact
to listen at a level that is worthy of a human
is one of the most difficult things in all the world.

You invite me to listen to the wonder and the wounds
of my own selfhood and to the wonder and wounds
of those whose lives I'm privileged
to reach out to and touch each day.

You provoke me into deeper ability to listen
at levels, which I hardly knew were there in me,
those deep and rich depths
of my human mystery and history.

Loving Lord,
how can I possibly listen to any other human being
unless first of all I'm ready, willing and able
to be listened to by you and to listen to you?

Give me a listening heart and mind, Lord,
a heart and mind to understand
all that you want to share with me.
Let me hear in the deepest depths of self
your understanding and your compassion,
your acceptance and your love,
your forgivingness and your trust.

The first person who has to learn to listen is my own self.
Loving, ever-present and ever-listening Lord,
give me the courage to become a better listener in depth
to all you would whisper into my mind and heart.

Denis Blackledge 1992

On entering church

Lord,
your house seems noisy,
people exchanging news, dates,
appointments;
such a hustle and bustle of busy-ness.
I want to be quiet, Lord,
why don't they stop?
Lord, why don't you stop them?
Drive them out
like the money-changers in the Temple?

Lord,
I've realised
it's not the noise around me
that distracts me and my prayers;
it's me, Lord,
my mind darting from one thing to another.
Did I turn down the oven?
Did I lock the door?
Is my hair tidy?
Does my dress really suit me?
How I wish I'd finished the ironing yesterday.
What shall I have for tea?
Am I ready for work next week?

Lord,
cast them out;
drive away the distractions to my worship;
all the thoughts that take my mind
from looking to you.
No, Lord,
it's not just the noise outside
that destroys,
but also the noise within.

Judith Stevens 1993

Prayer of confession

We're all different, Lord.

Different from each other,
and different within ourselves:
    sometimes joyful, sometimes sad;
    at times malicious, at other times kind;
    often angry, rarely at peace;
    usually trusting, yet shaken by doubt.

We thank you that we know you will come to us
    in different ways at different times.

You will help us to look at our anger,
    and use it for good;
you will take our peacefulness to calm others.

You will give us strength in our grief,
    and provide an unshakeable rock
    beneath all our doubts.

You will meet us in our worst moments of pride
    and egotism;
challenge us, and pick us up,
and set us again in the path of love.

You will follow us to the darkest places
    of our lives,
rescue us from our deepest sin,
and bring us to your presence and your love.

Again and again you will be to us
    the very spirit of love, and joy,
    and companionship.
Thanks be to you, Lord Jesus.

David Temple 1988

Prayers of adoration and confession

Leader	Why are you waiting, people of the living God?
All	We are waiting for his promises to be fulfilled.
Reader A	He is the God of power, he is the First, the Last. Creator, before the cosmos first began, it is he who is and shall be.
Reader B	He made galaxies and atoms, he made interstellar spaces, it was he who called to being living creatures, people, souls.
Reader A	He rages in the thunder, he splits mountains with his storm-clouds, he dances on each dust-mote and then gurgles with each baby.
Reader B	He is mother to the motherless, he is life to those who die, and by himself he promised, and by himself he spoke and said that he would be our Saviour, God of power and peace, the Lord!
Leader	Why are you waiting, people of the living God?
All	We are waiting for his promises to be fulfilled.
Reader A	He is the word, eternal, who did not cling to his privilege, for he comes to us a baby, born among a subject people.
Reader B	He became a poor girl's child, a refugee, an outcast,

        the worker who gave up his tools
        to challenge, heal and teach.

Reader A   He chose to be the homeless one,
        the convict, broken-bodied, who dragged evil
           down to hell
        and trod its dust beneath his feet.

Reader B   He's built the road out of our wilderness,
        he's flung wide the gates of freedom,
        he himself has been our Saviour, he is Christ
           the King, the Lord!

Leader   Why are you waiting, people of the living God?

All   We are waiting for his promises to be fulfilled.

Reader A   He is the Spirit, he is life, he is the breath within
           our body,
        he is fire and he is glory, he's the twist in DNA.

Reader B   It is he who shows us learning, it is he who
           teaches knowledge,
        he dams rivers, lights our houses,
        he heals with the hands of nurses.

Reader A   He converts and cures our souls,
        he breaks the bonds of race and nation,
        he fills pockets and then empties them for love
           of humankind:
        he makes us anew each morning, he is Saviour,
           Spirit, Lord!

Leader   Why are you waiting, people of the living God?

All   We are waiting for his promises to be fulfilled.

Reader A   The first we wait for is forgiveness.

Reader B	Our brother dies of cholera upon our television screens. Our sister screams her hatred in our city streets. Our father turned to vapour in our bright atomic sun. Our mother sleeps in doorways, dies, forgotten in a corner. Our children choke on ozone, and will farm a ruined earth.
Reader A	We seek forgiveness. We did not wish these things to happen, but did not prevent them.
Leader	We dwell in quiet luxury through unjust terms of trade. We seek the quiet life in face of prejudice and lies. Our taxes gird us round with weapons and with armies, but we do not care for Christ-like folk, the poor, the damaged. We drive our cars, we waste our food, we pour filth on the waters. We are involved in these sins, by our silence, by our weakness. (*to readers*) Do you turn from these things?
Readers	We do, God help us.
Leader	(*to congregation*) Do you turn from these things?
All	We do, God help us.
Leader	As he has promised, the Creator makes us new. As he has promised, the Son sets us free. As he has promised, the Spirit leads us into life. Come, we shall sin no more, but live for him.
All	Amen. Thanks be to God.

Vince Gilbert 1996

Tingle factor

Loving Lord,
you invite and excite me,
you refresh and delight me,
you are the tingle factor of my life,
bringing me ever-new awareness
of the wonder that surrounds me.
You touch me, Lord,
and your touch brings awe,
comfort, reverence, gentleness,
acceptance, tenderness, affection,
encouragement, warmth, friendship,
appreciation, gratitude and praise.

Loving Lord,
how great you are!
I thank you for the wonder of your being,
I thank you for the wonder of my being,

I thank you for the wonder of each human being,
I thank you for the wonders of your creation.
A shiver of awesome delight shakes my whole being
as I open my eyes and ears and mind and heart,
and taste and see just how much
you delight to be-with and do-for your creatures!

And it's in the ordinary and the everyday
that I begin to notice the extraordinary
and the special all around me
I'm surrounded by so many
of your signs of power and wisdom.

When I stop and look and listen
I begin to see afresh.
A misty dawn.
A golden sunset.
A snow-capped mountain.
A swirling sea.
A lark ascending.

A feast of colour.
A touch of love.
A glance of welcome.
A smile of tenderness.
A taste of heroism.
A life of humdrum service.
A face lined with experience.

Loving Lord, the litany and list of praise
is endless and deeply personal.
For each one of us is gifted with an ability
to grow in that basic tingle factor
that is written into the depths of our being.
Each one of us catches a beginning of joy and delight,
that every now and then leaves us speechless.
Pardon the expression, Lord,
but each of us has the capacity
to be gobsmacked by glory!
Each one of us has that tremendous gift
of being able to feel those 'Ah, gosh!' moments
that expand our horizons
and bring us closer to one another and to you.

Loving Lord,
any time is a good time to begin to grow
in the tingle factor.
But perhaps holiday times,
or retirement,
or when out of work,
are privileged moments to bask a little
in that basic gift of the tingle factor
which comes from your ever-present loving touch.

Denis Blackledge 1992

So many things I can't believe

There are so many things
I can't believe.

I can't believe
the universe
exists purely by chance,
without plan,
design or purpose.

I can't believe
the sum of human history
is nothing but a struggle,
where those best able to adapt
to changing circumstances
survive,
procreate
and die.

I can't believe
all striving after truth and beauty
is meaningless –
no moral values;
no evil to be resisted;
no good to be won.

I can't believe
all love,
compassion
and self-sacrifice
can be explained away
in purely biological terms.

I stand where
every human being stands,
on the edge of mystery,
unfathomed depths
unscaled heights
great burning questions

      vast unknowns . . .
. . . but still
I cannot
not believe
in God.

Blessed be God,
      whose ways
      are far beyond our ways;
      whose truth
      is so much greater than our truth;
      whose wisdom
      cannot be comprehended by our knowledge;
      whose love
      is the origin and renewal of all love
      and whose life
      is the source of all life.
      Blessed be God.

Edmund Banyard 1995

Being still

We come from a busy world,
Yet you command us to be still.
We come from a noisy world,
Yet you command us to be silent.

      We come in anxious mood,
      Yet you command us to be restful.
      We come in aggressive mood,
      Yet you command us to be peaceful.

      We come with aggressive words,
      Yet you command us to be peaceful.
      We come with anxious words,
      Yet you command us to be restful.

We come with noisy minds,
Yet you command us to be silent.
We come with busy minds,
Yet you command us to be still.

Bruce D. Thompson 1989

Why I never wash . . .

1 I was made to wash as a child.
2 People who wash are hypocrites – they reckon
  they are cleaner than others.
3 There are so many different kinds of soap, I could
  never decide which one was right.
4 I used to wash, but it got so boring so I stopped.
5 I still wash on special occasions like Christmas
  and Easter.
6 None of my friends wash.
7 I'm still young. When I'm older and have got a bit
  dirtier I might start washing.
8 I really don't have the time.
9 The bathroom's never warm enough.
10 People who make soap are only after your money.

Anon. 1989

Lord of life – feed me

Lord of life –
Feed me this day.
Lord of love –
Fill me this day.
Lord of light –
Lead me this day.
Lord of all –
Keep me in your way,
Now and forever.

Bruce D. Thompson 1990

Advent to Epiphany

Come as a girl

God above
Should you revisit us
Come as a girl.
Experience deprivation, segregation,
Monthly cramps;
Experience rhythmic labour pains
    on your way to a
    waterless
    doctorless
    gloveless
    bedless labour suite.

Like us
You will be a cheap labourer
Eating a 'tithe' of the global granary;
A mouthless reproduction laboratory
And the last legal illiterate share.

God below,
Long before you give them
The new decalogue cut into stone
That has no feelings;
Long before you let them
Set the law for us,
Consult your mother.

Helen Wangusa 1993
(*Uganda*)

Come Emmanuel

*'A virgin will conceive and bear a son, and he shall be
called Emmanuel', a name which means 'God is with us'.
(Matthew 1.23-24 REB)*

Come Emmanuel:
Disperse our darkness with your light;
Dispel our insensitivity with your compassion;
Diffuse our selfishness with your justice.

Come Emmanuel:
God with us in the mystery of a humble birth.
God with us in the horror of the cross.
God with us in the explosiveness of the resurrection.

Come Emmanuel:
Come, forgive our insensitivity;
Come, heal our divisions;
Come, plant seeds of love.

Come Emmanuel:
Come to our world;
Come to our Church;
Keep on coming into our lives,
To change and transform and renew.

Keep on coming, Emmanuel,
today and always.

Christine Jones 1995

The Way

I am The Way
The only Way.
In winter or summer, in peace or war
In all of creation
Come, follow me

I am The Way
The Way of Truth,
For heavy laden or light of heart
In all human feelings
Come, follow me

I am The Way
The Way of Life.
Through joy and sorrow, rough and smooth
In all of life
Come, follow me

I am The Way
The Way to God.
From childhood to adult, from birth to death
In all of your being
Come, follow me

Lesley Steel 1995

The call to worship

*The place and street names indicated: (italics) should be
substituted with local place/street names*

First Sunday

A   Break forth into shouts of joy, O people of this
          battered, weary city!
      For your comforter is coming to your aid,
      and he will build you up anew,
      and all the world shall shout his praises!
      There is light upon the mountains –
      sing his praises, all ye people!

Hymn
There's a light upon the mountains, and the day is at spring

B   Good News! For God has not abandoned this, his
          people.
      He has not deserted this, his city, this our bruised,
      beloved (*Norwich*).
      He comes,
      he calls us,
      to drive out the bad,
      build up the good,
      right here –
      in (*Dover Street*) and (*Doris Road*),
      in (*Porters Field*) and anywhere we go –
      He comes,
      he challenges,
      he leads us.

C   We light this Advent candle as a sign:
      God cares, God comes, God makes his world anew.

Second Sunday

A   Why spend your money on things of no value?
      Why gobble down food that does not satisfy?

Turn to the Lord whose word is the truth,
drink from his fountains of joy and delight!
He is Lord, the Almighty, the King of Creation –
sing his praises, all ye people!

Hymn
Praise to the Lord, the Almighty, the King of Creation

B   God sends us out as messengers,
as healers,
as those who live his life
in this his city,
in our bruised, beloved (*Norwich*).
We will find him on estates, in factories,
in worried shops and offices.
His is the truth to live by,
his is the word upon our lips,
his is the story we proclaim by daily living.

C   We light this Advent candle as a sign:
God speaks, his word is active in his world.

Third Sunday

A   Prepare the way of the Lord!
He is the light that comes to darkness,
he is the strength that comes to weakness,
he is the wind we hear approaching like a mighty roar
    of thunder.
The Lord is near!
Prepare his way, and
sing his praises, all ye people!

Hymn
*On Jordan's bank the Baptist's cry announces that the Lord
is nigh*

B   God comes, and soon, and very soon to this his city,

to our bruised, beloved (*Norwich*).
Sweep out the dusty corners,
root out all the cobwebs, sins and failures.
Can you withstand his challenge and his silent gaze?
His is the unkempt coat, the beard, the cardboard box
    for bed.
Turn back again to him, make ready,
wait for him,
he's knocking, knocking, knocking at your door.

C   We light this Advent candle as a sign:
    we shall make ready for his coming, he is closer than
        we think.

Fourth Sunday

A   Let the whole world keep silence!
    For the maker of creation's coming here,
    he brings his holy presence to our everyday.
    Glory! Glory!
    Sing his praises, all ye people!

Hymn
The angel Gabriel from heaven came

B   God comes,
    and such an unexpected coming.
    He is found among the weak,
    the poor,
    the lonely,
    the despised,
    the people we would never think of.
    He binds the very wounds of this, our bruised,
    beloved (*Norwich*).
    He comes, for us to find him,
    celebrate him in his weakness,
    in his model for our lives.

C   We light this Advent candle as a sign:
God comes, to those who least expect him,
to the ones who need him most.
We shall go there, where he is, to worship him.

Christmas Morning
(could also be used as part of a Midnight service)

A   A baby's born, and all the angels
kneel to pay him homage!
Sing his praises, all ye people!

Hymn
Hark! the herald angels sing

B   God comes,
he's born,
he's here.
And every brick and stone,
each building,
tree,
and every child of God,
is filled with heaven,
now and evermore.
Yes in this city,
in our bruised, beloved (*Norwich*),
he is here.

C   We light this Christmas candle as a sign:
God comes, is born, and all creation stops,
and holds its breath, and worships.

Vince Gilbert 1996

Still waiting

Loving Lord,
we are still waiting.
Advent reminds us
that we are perched between memory and dream.
The memory of your first coming.
The dream of your second coming.
Those early Christians at the end of
the first century
had a strong sense of your second coming,
had great expectations it could be very soon.
At the beginning of the twenty-first century
we have lost that edge, that bite,
that sense of readiness, that urgency
of the final coming of your kingdom
of justice, love and peace.

Loving Lord,
that is why we need Advent
to re-source ourselves,
to take us back to you as the source and goal
of all we are born to be.
We are an Advent People,
people of the dream.

And the essence of it all, Lord,
is that delicate balance
of being still
and being able to wait.
Only by a constantly renewed return
to you as source and centre of stillness
can there be an urgent opening up
to all that has to be undergone, sweated through,
suffered and worked at in the waiting
for the completion of your kingdom.

Loving Lord,
we have to be content to enter into
that groaning and travail of creation
as we become altogether new creatures
founded in and on you.
We have to be content to work at
our patch of the kingdom-garden,
with the patience of good growers
who sow seeds and let them be.

Loving Lord,
Advent takes us all back to our roots,
enables us to see with far-sighted eyes,
gives us new encouragement to move on
with that pilgrim journey as friends
and followers of the king who is to come . . .

Denis Blackledge 1992

The Annunciation

Did He who sent
the messenger
read 'yes'
within her
before
the Word was spoken
as
the world's salvation
poised
between
summons and reply
hung
on a woman's word?

Suppose her answer
had been negative
or none at all,
that her fame
for 'no'
had been remembered
and
only
magnified the problem
of the poor?

Had God no reservations
or reserve in mind,
another choice,
another town,
a different time
for

highly favoured blessing
or
burdening selectivity?
Then her acclaim
might be,
'hail, mother of anonymity'.

Mother of God
whose
psalm of affirmation
sings
the time is now,
this the acceptable day,
first to respond
' . . . as you have spoken
let it be . . .'
our pattern of consent
to God
the Word made flesh
in us . . .

Help us to
magnify the Lord
in our assent,
let it be
nothing
less
than
'yes'.

Kenneth Carveley 1989

Magnificat: the mystery of Mary

Lady, caught
     in swift surprise;
     mind spinning
     heart willing,
     grace by the Spirit
     in bearing
     the Body of your Son,
each day, each hour
help us say 'yes' to God.

Lady, lying
     with your child
     close
     to God
     and man,
     offering care
     for
     the Body of your Son,
each life, each love
help glorify the Lord.

Lady, worrying
     like us,
     anticipating loss,
     searching
     unknowing
     in the Father's house
     the new Temple
       new Jerusalem,
     the Body of your Son,
each change, each loss,
help us to find the Lord.

Lady, how sure
     you ask
     in confidence
     of being heard
     and of His will,

sustaining
prayer
in the Body of your Son,
each time, each place,
help us to seek the Lord.

Lady, outside
the door,
perplexed –
as
He fills the hungry
with good things,
and the rich
go empty away
– yet not displaced
in letting go,
and others in
the Body of your Son,
each question, each uncertainty
help us to trust the Lord.

Lady, standing by
but no bystander
at the Cross
can feel as you
the piercing
in
watching
and cradling
the Body of your Son,
each hurt, each pain,
help us to love the Lord.

Lady, living
with us
your new people
in our life,

as
here and there
we catch
a glimpse of you
in
the Body of your Son,
each joy, each hope,
help us to magnify the Lord.

Kenneth Carveley 1988

Angels

Flames of fire, shafts of illumination;
Disconcerting messengers of God;
Assuring a woman that she can give birth,
Telling a man that what she bears is
Gift from God; challenging us to
Look, and not seek life where only death
Is found; opening doors, surrounding us with
Care, surprising us into fresh understanding.

Ann Lewin 1991

He came to his own home

Christmas Eve (John 1.11)

Bright moon, scattered stars;
so solitary is creation.
The universe which God has created is especially silent on
    this night.
It waits with bated breath for the Lord of Creation to return.
The universe belongs to God, it is his home.

Silence reigns supreme.
The flowers of the field sway gently in the moonlight.
This night, the vast earth awaits the homecoming of our
    Creator God.
The vast earth and open fields belong to God, they are his
home.

Bethlehem lies dreaming.
In his gentle mother's arms, the babe sleeps peacefully
    this night.
The City of David awaits the homecoming of David's
    descendant.
The town of Bethlehem belongs to him, it is his home.

My bones, my flesh, my blood, my lungs and my heart,
were all made by his hand.
This night, my heart is at peace, awaiting my Creator's return.
My heart belongs to him, it is his home.

Wang Weifan 1991

Carol for a dark age

To the tune of 'God rest you merry gentlemen'

God challenge and awaken us
who share this joyful feast
to celebrate the birth of Christ,
our Saviour, Lord and Priest;
who came the light of love to shed
on greatest and on least –

O lighten our darkness with your love –
with your love.

Where terrorists still use the power
of fear of bomb and gun,
Where children play in ruined streets
and think that fighting's fun;
where war and famine kill a child
when life has just begun –

O lighten . . .

Where people doss in doorways, or
the mortgage can't be paid;
where being made redundant leaves
folk aimless and afraid;
where children take the consequence
of evils we have made –

O lighten . . .

Where we are still indifferent to
the cry of human pain;
where profit's all important
and we only think of gain;
then Saviour Christ, this Christmas, in
our hearts be born again –

O lighten . . .

Rosemary Wakelin 1992

Round the back in Bethlehem

Matthias the innkeeper had had a rotten day. Bethlehem was crammed with visitors; his best rooms were commandeered by Roman officials who demanded room service and bossed everyone around; the grand Sadducees who had booked them first were blaming him and bossing everyone around except the Romans; and a group of Pharisees wanted hot and cold running water to wash away the defilement of such a mixed collection of travellers. Everyone else was boasting about being descended from King David, or grumbling that Royal David's City was nothing like the pictures in the brochures. There was even a party of foreigners from some northern island, muttering through long droopy moustaches about holly and ivy and mistletoe, whatever that was. To cap it all, Caesar Augustus had decreed that the whole world should be taxed bang in the bleak mid-winter. Snow had fallen, snow on snow, and people were tramping the stuff all over his nice clean floors.

At last he had closed the bar, and seen the last customers off to bed, saying, with as much grace as he could muster, 'God rest ye merry gentlemen . . .' He climbed upstairs, and with a short but fervent prayer for a silent night, tumbled into bed.

Hardly had his head touched the pillow when, ding dong merrily, the doorbell rang. Down he went, to find a bedraggled couple with an arthritic donkey.

'Sorry, no room,' he snapped.

The man looked so downcast that Matthias did not immediately slam the door in their faces. He caught the kind brown eye of the donkey and seemed to detect a jerk of its head towards the back of the inn.

'Oh, all right,' he said, 'you can share the stable with your donkey. You'd better sign the register. Name?'
'Joseph,'
'Occupation?'
'Carpenter.'
'You one of those born of David's line then?'
'Oh yes,' answered Joseph. 'David begat Solomon, and Solomon begat Rehoboam, and Rehoboam begat Abijah,

and Abijah begat Jehoshaphat and Jehoshaphat . . .'
'Never mind all that,' said Matthias. 'I'd better get you a couple
of blankets. The earth's as hard as iron out there, and water's
like a stone.'
'You mean we must spend the night where oxen feed on hay?'
asked Mary.
'Don't worry,' said Joseph. 'At least it'll be quiet away in a
manger.'

So the innkeeper settled back into bed while they took the
donkey and the blankets round the back.

He had just snuggled down when a tremendous burst of
singing filled the room. Cursing noisy neighbours, he tried to
make out where it came from. It seemed to be up in the sky,
and it was all about Peace on Earth.

'Fat lot of peace here,' he muttered, feeling very little goodwill
towards anyone. But eventually the music faded and he dozed off.

It felt like half a minute later when the doorbell rang again.
He shot downstairs. A collection of shepherds stood outside.
'We're looking for . . .' they started.
'No lost sheep here,' he growled.
'That's as may be. We were watching our flocks by night,
all seated on the ground, when . . .'
'Get on with it! What are you looking for?'
'Oh, ah,' they answered. 'A lowly cattle shed.'
'Well, I've got a shed round the back, but it's got people in it.'
'We know. That's why we're here. You see, we bring glad
tidings of great . . .'
Matthias had had enough.
'Round the Back!' he shouted and slammed the door.

Back in bed he tried counting sheep, thinking at last 'All is
calm', when suddenly all was bright. There was a whoosh,
and his room was filled with light. He dashed to the window,
looked up, and saw a star, just moving round the corner to the
back of the inn. He was still looking out, when he saw some
camels approaching.

'This really is the limit,' he fumed. 'It must be past three
o'clock.'

He stamped downstairs, flung open the door and bellowed,
'Do you know what time it is?'
'Well,' said a voice. 'According to our calculation, we rather
think it's the dawn of a new era.'
'Wise guys, eh?' said Matthias through gritted teeth.
'You could say that,' said another. 'But actually we three kings
of Orient are. Bearing gifts . . .'
'Well, you can't park your camels there.'
'Where then?' asked a third voice.
'Round the Back!' he bellowed.

Just then, Joseph re-appeared through the snow, which
was now deep and crisp and even.
'Er, can I have another blanket, please? The ox and ass
are doing their best, but it's still pretty cold for the baby.'
'Baby?' gasped Matthias. 'That's all I need!'
'You're right there,' said Joseph, with a weary smile.

Sore affrayed and grievously bewildered, Matthias fetched
another blanket and stamped round the back, shouting
'Here's your blankety blanket!' when he was stopped in his
tracks by a dozen pairs of eyes staring at him. Everyone was
clustered round, full reverently on bended knee.
'Hark!' whispered a herald angel. 'This is the first Nowell,
and we're hailing the Heaven-born Prince of Peace. So come,
let us adore him.'
'W-What on earth are you talking about?' spluttered Matthias.
A shepherd dug him in the ribs and said,
'Calm down, mate. It's tidings of comfort and joy; you'll see,'
and nodded towards the manger.

There was the baby, all neatly wrapt in swathing bands. As
the innkeeper tucked the blanket around the child, his scowl
vanished. When Mary smiled her thanks, he suddenly felt very
small. He went and knelt behind the kneeling donkey, in the
dark, round the back.

That is why you never see him in the Nativity pictures.

Adrian Stokes 1995

Incarnation

He's grown, that Baby,
Not that most people have noticed.
He still looks the same,
Lying there in the straw, with
Animals and shepherds looking on.
He's safe there, locked in that moment
Where time met Eternity.

Reality of course is different,
He grew up, astonished people with his
Insight, disturbed them with
Ideas that stretched them into
New maturity

Some found him
Much too difficult to cope with,
Nailed him down to fit their
Narrow minds

We are more subtle.
Keep him helpless,
Refuse to let him be the Man he is,
Adore him as the Christmas Baby,
Eternally unable to grow up
Until we set him free.

By all means let us pause there
At the stable, and
Marvel at the miracle of birth.
But we'll never get to know
God with us, until we learn
To find him at the Inn,
A fellow guest who shares the joy and sorrow,
The Host who is the life we celebrate.

He's grown, that Baby.

Ann Lewin 1991

A child's prayer at the crib

Dear Lord
Shepherds came to you
Kings came to you following a star;
it led them right to you.
There you were sleeping in the hay

amongst all the cows, donkeys and sheep.
They were surprised to see
such an important person
in such humble surroundings.

Lord you taught us
that however much wealth we have
we are all the same
and that no one should treat one person
with more respect than others.

Thank you dear Lord.

Amen

Eva Ratcliffe (aged 9) 1987

Christmas Communion

This table is our Bethlehem, the holy place to which the star
  guides us.
> It is the place where we see the glory of God.
> It is the place where for us peace from
>> God's own heart is given to the earth.
> It is the place to which we bring our shepherding,
>> the duties and responsibilities of our lives,
>>> that they may be gathered up into the mystery and
>>>> miracle and meaning of the incarnation.
> It is the place to which we bring all human learning
>> and riches and kingship that they may be made
>>> holy.
> It is the place to which we bring our gifts of bread and
>> wine
>> that God may become incarnate for us.
> It is the place where we celebrate in sign and symbol
>> the whole story of our faith.

Michael Powell 1987

Christmas

Holy Child of Bethlehem,
    whose parents found no room in the inn;
    we pray for all who are homeless.

Holy Child of Bethlehem,
    born in a stable;
    we pray for all who live in poverty.

Holy Child of Bethlehem,
    rejected stranger;
    we pray for all who are lost, alone,
    all who cry for loved ones.

Holy Child of Bethlehem,
    whom Herod sought to kill;
    we pray for all who live with danger,
    all who are persecuted.

Holy Child of Bethlehem,
    a refugee in Egypt;
    we pray for all who are far from their homes.

Holy Child of Bethlehem,
    in you the Eternal was pleased to dwell,
    help us, we pray, to see the divine image
    in people everywhere.

David Blanchflower 1987

After Christmas

The stable is empty now,
Echoes of forgotten moments are all that remain.
A baby's cry, the tears of a mother's joy,
All are gone.
Just another stable – dark, cold, unwelcoming,
Not the place we'd choose . . . and yet,
It was here that poverty found its master,
Oppression its freedom.
Here humanity stood, face to face with God,
       and creation was reborn.
Here love's victory began.
The stable is empty now . . . but the world is filled.

G. M. Breffitt 1987

Twelfth Night

It looks much as it did before,
Now that the cards and decorations
Have come down.
The furniture of life is back in place,
The old routine takes over.
But are we the same?
Is there no echo of the angels' song
Lifting our spirits, no stillness
In our hearts, reminding us that
We were there, just for a moment,
At that birth,
Catching a glimpse of glory?
Let's not put that away,
Tangled with tinsel, for another time.
Let's ponder in our hearts, like Mary,
And let the child grow with us
Through the year.

Ann Lewin 1991

Lent and Passion

Ash Wednesday

Keep in mind that you are dust
    and unto dust you shall return.
Indeed Lord, you've given us a transitory world,
A world whose beauty is expressed in huge variety,
    the subtly-altering tints of dawn and dusk,
    the many-hued rhythms of the seasons,
    the crisscrossing ripples on the
        surface of quiet pools.
And we? We spend our time trying to carve
    permanent niches for ourselves,
    furnishing desirable long-term residences
    with things which give us value
        in our own eyes.

Keep in mind that you are dust
    and unto dust you shall return.
The glories of the world around
    escape our notice by and large.
Songbirds' nests are not quoted
        on the Stock Exchange;
    so root out the hedgerows
    in the name of economic viability.
Where your treasure is,
    there your heart is too.

Keep in mind that you are dust
    and unto dust you shall return.
You wanted to know what it is like
    to live in an impermanent world,
    or why would you have taken flesh like us?
The fragile structures could not hold you,
    yet you stayed within their grasp
        until your time came.

Breathing forth your Spirit into this world
    you left us to ponder,

'Let not your hearts be troubled,
    I have overcome.'
Keep in mind that you are dust
    and unto dust you shall return

Hilda Mary r.a. 1987

Palm Sunday

'Who is this?' people asked (Matthew 21.10)

Across the ages ring two cries
    conflicting,
    yet woven together,
'Blessings on him who comes in the name of the Lord!'
'Crucify him!'
Linked to the end of time
    by twisted human nature
    both wanting
    and rejecting God.
In a moment of history
    Jesus enters Jerusalem
    and goes to Calvary;
yet those events belong to every age,
    and in every age
    we shout 'Hosanna!'
    and are consenting to his death.

Lord, you come as one
    who has a rightful claim upon us
    yet without pomp,
    or weapons or intrigue.
Riding a donkey
    you are ready to be laughed at,
    scorned, beaten, crucified.
you know what we are
    and what the end must be
    yet still you come.
Your foolishness confounds our wisdom.
Your weakness overthrows our strength.
You reach out towards us in love.
A love so easy to deny,
    so hard to escape,

we fail you, we reject you,
we have no claim upon you.
Yet still you claim us,
    and for your love's sake we dare to pray,
'Remember us, and save us into your Kingdom'.

Edmund Banyard 1987

Tears

Lord of life, you shared our life, you knew the grief of tears . . .
    Not gentle tears that trickle down the cheek
    at some lost memento, or last year's romance;
    not for you the easy tears mopped up and tossed aside
    in a soggy man-sized tissue . . .

For you, the weeping over Jerusalem
    you came to your own and they would not accept you;
    you loved them to the end and they rejected you;
    you mothered like a mother-hen her chicks but they
    would not have you.
And you wept . . .
    tears of rejection, for they would not respond to your
        love
    while you saw the end of those you loved so dearly
Still you say: Follow me, take up my cross, weep with me.

For you, the weeping at Lazarus' grave . . .
    you loved him too, he was your friend
There you wept . . .
    not for him alone
    but for humankind, captive
    to death and disease, hurt and pain, disintegration
        and destruction
    the enemy's great weapon against your loved creation
    the last affirmation of our first sin.
Still you say: Follow me, take up my cross, weep with me.

For you the weeping in the garden . . .
    as we could never weep, great drops of blood falling to
        the ground
    how deeply you loved, how deeply you felt the burden
        of our sin
    how costly the price of our salvation.
    'Let this cup pass from me' such is the pain
    'Not my will be done' such is the cost . . .
Still you say: Follow me, take up my cross, weep with me.

To weep over the city, corrupt, polluted and condemned
to weep over the grave, feared, inexorable.
To weep at the place of our sacrifice
    this
    is to share the suffering of our Lord.

David J. Ford 1997

Good Friday

Good Friday
And they had it right,
Not us!
Churches bare,
Tables stripped,
Unadorned,
And everything sombre –
Even though
We know in faith
How the story will unfold.

At the graveyard,
Cemetery,
What you will . . .
People were busy with trowel and secateur,
Oasis and watering can,
and the place was ablaze
With daffodils!

They had it right.
This is where we celebrate our dead,
with lament perhaps,
But certainly with flowers:
Whatever we call today
Death is Easter-place.

Edwina Sherrington 1989

Women and the Cross

For Good Friday (or other occasions) in the light of the ecumenical decade 'Churches in Solidarity with Women' 1989–1999.

The anointing woman
(Mark 14.1-11)

I am the woman who anointed Jesus.
He said the whole world would remember me
    for my actions.
    (but the men who wrote the gospels
    forget to tell you my name)
He knew what I wanted to do –
    better than I knew myself –
Every time I heard him speak,
    everything I heard him say,
    was so different from the world –
    so strange, so gentle, so peaceful –
    that I knew they would have to kill him:
    you could hear the coming suffering
    in all he did and said.

I ached to hear him and I longed
    to help him, get him ready,
    make the preparations
    for what he knew was on its way.

It cost everything I had – everything –
    every penny, every tear,
    every energy and hope –
    and I poured it all over him, preparing him:
    till the room swam with the fragrance.

They were all embarrassed and very quiet,
    one of them was very annoyed at the expense,
        but I couldn't help it:
    I just wiped it away with my hair –

and he accepted it.
I can smell it still.

Someone had to help him be ready,
 someone had to care as much as he did.
 Women like me know what it means
 to be hated by the world –
 a man like that is offering
 the death and burial of such hate:
 the funeral of the world and the birth –
 alive and fresh –
 of something strange and gentle and peaceful.

The serving woman
(Luke 22.54-61)

I am the serving woman
 in the courtyard by the fire.
I was serving the men who arrested this Jesus –
 they wanted a drink while the High Priest
 worked out what to do with him:
 we could see them inside
 through the doorway.
I recognised his friend,
 though he wasn't saying much
 just keeping his distance;
 near enough to see –
 and to keep warm –
 but not near enough to be involved
 or let us see the fear in his eyes.

I felt sorry for him.
I wondered what it was about this Jesus,
 that earned such fear and such devotion.
I spoke to his friend, to help really,
 but he swore at me –
 and at himself –
 and said they weren't friends.

I watched him as he got more agitated –
    and I watched Jesus standing there inside
    so still, so silent and so sad.
But it was the last moment
    I shall never forget,
    printed always on my mind, my heart,
    just after his friend again denied knowing him,
    just before he ran off into the night,
    sobbing his heart out.
Jesus turned round and looked at him.

They were still slapping him,
    spitting at him, jeering:
    but he was looking for his friend.
I know – I know what that look meant:
    it meant need and pain, yes,
    but it also meant mercy and pity
    and even forgiveness:
I was shocked, shaken.
    He wasn't only looking at his friend
    but at me too – and everyone else.
He was looking at us all
    in need and in pain –
    at us all
    in mercy and in pity and forgiveness.

Pilate's wife
(Matthew 27.12-22)

I am the wife of the Roman Governor.
I saw him once, this Jesus,
    heard him speaking in the city –
    only once, but his voice and his face
    have haunted me, into my sleep, my dreams:
    the words he spoke, the way he spoke them,
    the strength, the quietness and the innocence.

My husband is the Governor,
    sitting in the judgement seat,
    but this man judges him,

judges all of us, the city,
the empire, his own people.

I dreamed of justice and of innocence
and it was this man saying 'mercy':
'happy are the merciful and the peaceful
and the poor', he said.

And in my dream his clear words
cut my darkness into two –
the darkness of power and cruelty and violence,
the confusion of anger and pride and exploitation,
the turmoil of ugliness and war and hunger . . .

I woke in fear and tears and ran to Pilate:
we have to let him go I said,
set him free with his message:
you can't crucify justice.

But he sat on his judgement seat
and let himself be judged.
Somehow we have to set him free.

The weeping women
(*Luke 23.26-33*)

We are the weeping women of Jerusalem.
We've seen enough crucifixions to harden us
but this was different.
We followed him out of the city –
some of us had followed him before –
we all knew about him,
had heard him, seen him.
We watched him stagger
till they got someone else to carry his cross:
he said there would be a cross to carry,
a cross inside – like a baby –
as well as this one on his shoulder.
He seemed to be carrying such a weight,
he seemed to soak up all they did to him

and hold it –
hold onto it, like drawing out a poison.
He staggered on with it.

He spoke to us –
like a great heaving sigh
he told us to dry our tears:
not to cry for him but for ourselves,
for our children.
He could see where this cruelty
and viciousness leads –
on till we destroy ourselves,
till we are so dry and brittle
the fire of hate will consume us in a second's flash.

But we cried all the more
till we couldn't see
his stumbling back for tears:
he went on, on to the hill,
and all the way up he soaked up more,
drawing it all onto himself,
taking it with him,
up and on to that cross on the top of the hill.

We cry for ourselves,
because we have helped to put him there –
we cry for him because he seems
to be taking all the blame:
taking it all,
up there, with him on the cross.

The women at the cross
(*Mark 15.33-41*)

We are the women who waited at the cross.
We had to stand at a distance
and had to watch –
but we were not going away,
not going to let him die entirely alone,
entirely un-mourned.
We had followed him this far,

heard him, watched him, helped him,
we were his friends,
somehow we wanted to stand by him.

Yet in all the noise and shouting,
through the swearing and the cursing,
the banging and the groaning;
across the distance between us,
in the deepening darkness,
even in the frightening, shocking,
loneliness of his last cry,
even then
we did not feel we were giving him anything:
he was giving to us – still;
we stood by him, at a distance,
to find that he was standing by us,
alongside us, inside us,
his shadow within us.

He suffered the worst we could do to him –
deserting him,
hurting him,
forgetting him,
ignoring him –
and he lets us –
he lets us, somehow,
so that when we have done it to him
we will not need to do it to anyone else
ever again.

His last scream took something away,
for ever,
we watched and waited and did nothing –
and yet everything is changed.

The mother
(John 19.23-30)

I am the woman, Mary, his mother.
I did not always understand my son –

he never married to give me grandchildren,
he left home and job
to wander with his friends,
he put other loyalties above his family
and talked of sharing one father
with all the world.
I did not always understand him.

But this I understand –
    this suffering and this death.
As much as it hurts
        I know it isn't unexpected:
    he knew that living as he did,
    loving as only he could do,
    healing, teaching, blessing, giving
    as only he can do
    would stir a bitter hatred
    that only he could cure.

And only this way could he cure it.

But I am his mother
        and remember the longing and
        the aching for his birth –
        a grief that waited to be turned to joy.
And now I long to take him in my arms again
        and hold him in his anguish –
        a mother bringing him to birth again.

I am learning
        as he gives his friend into my care,
        and me to his,
        that all the future
        is this nurturing and nursing
        of each other to a new birth.

Mary Magdalene
(John 27.57-61)

I am the woman Mary of Magdala,
        the one they call the prostitute.

I loved him –
every way it's possible to love him
    and I haven't stopped. I can't.

Now that all the shouting and the banging,
    all the waiting and the weeping,
    all the darkness and groaning is over –
now that we gather the spices for his body,
    the linen and the ointment,
now I know –
    quietly inside and certainly –
    the love is growing still:
    aching, crying, mystified –
    but it doesn't go away.

He said so himself.
The little seed that falls –
falls for love –
    into dark earth – it doesn't die,
    like the seed in the womb,
    it broods for a harvest to come.
For now we only have
    the last, forlorn gestures of affection –
    to trim his body,
    dress his corpse and so to say farewell.

For me, for women like me, and for men,
    for everyone,
    there is no way backwards now
back past the healing barrier of his love:
    only quietly forward,
    puzzled but determined,
looking for a movement of the seed,
    waiting,
    for a harvest-breaking of the earth.

Simon Bailey 1989

The stones cry out . . .

Jesus
the stones cry out
along the road you tread
and as you pass through city street,
with cross-beam on your back,
they feel the weight of all the sins you take for us
cry out in anguish at the load you bear.

Jesus
the stones cry out
at the burning of tears
shed by women along your way,
seeing you, their friend,
suffering 'neath the load you carry;
and as you stop and take their pain,
they cry out again for yet more weight they bear.

Jesus
the stones cry out
as you stumble and fall,
and as the lashing of whip
beats upon your back,
and taunt and jeers
add to the load of sin and hate,
they cry out again for yet more pain you bear.

Jesus
the stones cry out
as soldiers beat and drive you to Calvary's hill
where you will die for me;
and as cruel spikes are driven
through hands and feet,
the stones cry out and echo
striking hammer on nail.

Jesus
the stones cry out
in answer to your anguished cry –
'It is finished' echoes down the years,
and still they cry out;
the Son of God has passed, here, by,
and brought salvation for all,
and for me.

Ernest Smart 1988

Cross-carrying Jesus: a prayer of confession

As you stagger on your lonely journey
time slips
worlds reel.
Forgive us that we turn away
embarrassed
uncaring
despairing.
Help us to stay with you through the dark night
to watch and to wait
to know the depths of your anguish
and to realise that you carry us
forgive (even) us
love us.
Forgive us
that we get on with our work unthinking
that we gamble unknowing with precious things.
Cross-carrying Jesus
nailed to the tree of life
forgive us
and grant us your salvation.

Kate McIlhagga 1988

This is the day they call good

This is the day they call good.

On this day they call good, they took a man. A man like no other man before or since. A man they did not understand. A man who spoke the truth. A man who gave offence. A man who denounced. A man who spoke the truth even when it hurt. A man who loved. A man who defended the poor. A man who healed the sick. A man who touched the untouchable. A man who befriended the prostitutes but did not make use of them. A man of integrity. A man they did not understand.

This is the day they call good.

On this day they call good, they killed a man. They stripped the man naked. They beat the man with iron-tipped whips till the blood flowed free. They vilified the man. They degraded the man. They abused the man. They rammed the thorns of a caricature crown deep into his skull.

This is the day they call good.

On this day they call good, they tied the man to a rough hewn wooden cross. They drove nails through his wrists and ankles deep into the wooden beams. The sound of ripping flesh drowned by the shouts of 'Crucify!' The pain of the rough, cold iron tearing through sinew and vein dulled by the throbbing ache in every part of his body. The passage of the nails lubricated by his own blood flowing freely.

This is the day they call good.

On this day they call good, the man was frightened. As he had prayed in the garden to be freed from his fate he was anguished and afraid. It had been easy in that bright, warm room to say that he had already been anointed for burial. So easy to be brave then. Anointed now by his own sweat, blood and tears he was terrified. As he hung there he was filled with dread, aghast that he had been abandoned. He cried out in fear: 'My God, my God why did you abandon me?'

This is the day they call good.

On this day they call good, all was not in vain. He bore the torment. He withstood the scorn. He endured the pain. He suffered in silence almost to the end. Not because he wanted to. But because he knew he had to. Not because it was pointless, mindless violence that was being inflicted on him. But because he understood the point of it all too well. Our sin.

This is the day they call good.

On this day they call good, he suffered with such seeming dignity that a pagan soldier, not one of the chosen people, the children of God, cried 'Truthfully, this man was a son of God.'

This is the day they call good.

On this day they call good, they crucified a man and revealed our God.

That is why we call this day good.

Ron Reid 1997

Meditation – nails

(*Matthew 2.1-18*)

My name is Meliakim. I work metal. Have done for years.
Usually on Friday you'd find me in my shop, smelting down
the ore, forging the metal. Nails. That's my bread and butter.
Nice little contract for nails, with the Romans.
Usually you'd find me there about this time on a Friday.

But not today. Oh no. I've waited too long for this, lain awake
too many nights, cried too many tears.
And all because of you, Jesus. The Christ!

He'd be about your age now, if he'd lived.
Ironic isn't it? We'd called him Joshua too, just like you.
'The Lord saves'.
The Lord saves? How did he save our Joshua? Where was his
saving power when the soldiers came in the night, burst into
our room brandishing swords and clubs, and killed him before
our eyes?
God almighty, he wasn't even two years old!

It was only later I learned that Herod had ordered all the boys
under two in our district to be killed.
We lived in Bethlehem then, and Herod had been told a child
who would be King had been born there. Red rag to a bull.

Such misery I have never seen.
They say the blood ran red in the streets for that boy.
They say the screams of the mothers could be heard the other
side of the Jordan.

I vowed that night I would see that child die.

My wife never recovered from the shock.
She died delivering our second child. The child was stillborn.

And since that day over 30 years ago, my whole life has been
eaten up with bitterness towards the child born to be King.

So finally, here we are. Face to face.
I watched the soldiers hammer the nails – **my** nails – into his
left hand and I cried out **'that's for my son!'**
And when the nail – **my** nail – went through his right hand,
I cried **'that's for my wife!'**
It's strange, I thought I would gloat.
I thought I would feel some great surge of satisfaction.
But when he heard me cry out he raised his head.
It was the first time I'd really looked at his face.
He didn't look like I expected. I thought he'd be proud,
self-satisfied, smug even. Most Kings are – oblivious to the
suffering they've inflicted, cushioned from how they make their
people suffer.
But he wasn't.

There was more suffering etched on his face than you
can imagine.
Not just his own suffering – God knows that was bad enough.
No, somehow he seemed to be carrying . . . carrying the
suffering of the world.

My suffering.

I looked at the nails. I thought of how I'd worked them in
the forge.
Red hot, white hot. And suddenly I felt the same heat, red
hot, white hot, surge through my breast – and all the bitterness
of the years was burned away, in one unbelievable moment.
I closed my eyes and gasped.

The power of the moment had taken me by surprise. I did not
think it possible to forgive and be forgiven in the same instant.
But that's what had happened.

When I opened my eyes he was dead.

Adrian Newman 1997

Dying Stranger

Dying Stranger
your arms stretch wide
and draw my wretched life
within the compass of your innocence.

My deeds of violence
become as nought
when by this miracle of grace
you work a work of resurrection power
and offer even me the life I threw away.

My days of waste and wantonness
are lost like rain upon the sea
when from your lips you speak my name
and circle me with unexpected hope.

My words of cruelty and hate
are suddenly eclipsed –
when in the noontide darkness on the hill
You bathe with light my dying breath
and take away my pounding guilt
with promises of Paradise.

Are you a madman or a god?
Delirious or divine?
Why do you move my eyes to tears?
You're right, my friend;
Heaven is at hand
and Paradise today.

David Jenkins 1988

Powerful silence

They whipped Him
They stripped Him of His clothes and . . .
He never said a word.

Thorns pierced His flesh
Blood ran down His face and . . .
He never said a word.

They spat in His face
They beat Him over the head and . . .
He never said a word.

They crucified Him
Drove vicious nails through His hands and feet and . . .
He never said a word.

In silence He earned *my* forgiveness
In silence He showed how much He loves me
What can I say?

Sheelah Stevens 1988

Holy Saturday

Wait, my friends, it is not over yet;
   the dark hours slowly move,
how slowly they move.
He is dead: my Lord, my hope.
   And darkness still hold sway.

Tomorrow sunshine may come,
   but today . . . today I wait;
   I wait with those who still must wait;
I sorrow with those deep in sorrow;
   my tears are for those who weep;
I stand in emptiness with all those whose life
   is a lonely waste,
   a void of nothingness;
All who know the pain of parting death.

Mothers stand helpless and watch their
   children die
   through bullet, bomb, pollution,
   empty bellies, unknown terrors,
as Mary stood and watched her own son die.

And I stand by, too, and let them kill
   by force, by greed,
   by necessary cuts,
   by blind belief,
As Pilate, too, stood idly by and watched them
   go to Calvary.

And as I watch them lay him in
   the tomb,
   I know . . .
   I know why darkness fills the land,
   I know why darkness fills the world:
   My Lord, my hope is dead.
   God is no more!
Will tomorrow ever come?

O Lord, I watch by your dark tomb;
Watch, I pray by the dark tomb of my despair.

My sins have put you there:
    Sins of doing
    sins of being
    sins of not doing
    sins of not being . . .
Tomorrow, if you should rise
take away my sin,
take away the sin of the world . . .

But today I wait in darkness . . .

David Blanchflower 1988

In search of a roundtable

Concerning the why and how and what
and who of ministry,
One image keeps surfacing:

A table that is round.

It will take some sawing
to be roundtabled,
some redefining
and redesigning.
Some redoing and rebirthing
of narrowlong Churching
can painful be
for people and tables.
It would mean no daising
and throning,
for but one king is there,
and He was a footwasher,
at table no less.

And what of narrowlong ministers
when they confront
a roundtable people,
after years of working up the table
to finally sit at its head,
only to discover
that the table has been turned round?

They must be loved into roundness,
for God has called a People,
not 'them and us'.
'Them and us'
are unable
to gather round,
for at a roundtable,
there are no sides
and *all* are invited
to wholeness and to food.

At one time
our narrowlong churches
were built to resemble the cross
but it does no good
for buildings to do so,
if lives do not.

Roundtabling means
no preferred seating,
no first and last,
no better, and no corners
for the 'least of these'.
Roundtabling means
being with,
a part of,
together, and one.
It means room for the Spirit
and gifts
and disturbing profound peace for all.

We can no longer prepare for the past.

We will and must and are called
to be Church,
and if He calls for other than roundtable
we are bound to follow.

Leaving the sawdust
and chips, designs and redesigns
behind,
in search of and in the presence of
the kingdom
that is His and not ours.

Chuck Lahrop 1988
(*Reproduced from* The Good Wine *by Josephine Bax,*
Church House Publishing, 1986)

To women and to men

O Eternal Wisdom,
we praise you and give you thanks,
because the beauty of death could not contain you.
You broke forth from the comfort of the grave;
before you the stone was moved,
and the tomb of our world was opened wide.
For on this day you were raised in power
and revealed yourself to women
as a beloved stranger,
offering for the rituals of the dead
the terror of new life
and of desire fulfilled.

Therefore, with the woman who gave you birth,
the women who befriended and fed you,
who argued with you and touched you,
the woman who anointed you for death,
the women who met you, risen from the dead,
and with all your lovers throughout the ages,
we praise you, saying,

Holy, holy, holy,
resurrection God,
heaven and earth are full of your glory;
hosanna in the highest.

Blessed is our brother Jesus,
who walks with us the road of our grief,
and is known again in the breaking of bread;
who, on the night he was handed over,
took bread, gave thanks, broke it, and said:
'This is my body, which is for you.
Do this to remember me.'
In the same way also the cup, after supper, saying:
'This cup is the new covenant in my blood.
Do this whenever you drink,
to remember me.'

Christ has died.
Christ is risen.
Christ will come again.

Come now, disturbing spirit of our God,
breathe on these bodily things
and make us one body in Christ.
Open our graves, unbind our eyes, and name us here:
touch and heal all that has been buried in us,
that we need not cling to our pain,
but may go forth with power
to release resurrection in the world.

Janet Morley 1988
(*Reproduced from* All Desires Known, *SPCK, 1992*)

The supper

This was a service which used much chart music as background to the prayers and readings leading up to the communion. The music used behind this particular part, where the words were set to the rhythm of the music, was called U got 2 Know (à la carte Paris mix) by the band Capella (LC7654) but other music could be used, such as many other Rave pieces, or Gregorian chants.

Bread and Wine
Mystical symbols of a world gone by
Strange and Wonderful
The man led out to die
But he's not in another world
Far beyond the veil
He's here and now
In you and me
And we live out his tale
Two millennia ago
This man walked the earth
Two thousand years later
We still cause his death
For this man was different
Beyond our understanding
He died
Yet rose again to life
And among us he is standing

This meal is not a bygone event
But is for us
And heaven sent

Welcome
Terrorist
Prostitute
Fisherfolk
Tax Collector
Thief
Betrayer

The Jesus folk

Welcome
Homeless
Unemployed
Made a joke
Greedy
Abused
Scandalised
Today's folk

God's gifts for God's people
Come Spirit
The bread we break
And wine we take
Reminds us of Jesus

The power of symbol
Of body and blood
Says to us all:
Jesus

Jesus took bread
Broke it and said . . .
'This is my body for you'

Jesus took cup
And lifted it up
'The new covenant in my blood'

Lamb of God who takes away sins
have mercy on us
Lamb of God who takes away sins
give us peace

Take it and eat it
This is a symbol of the Christ-man
Take it and drink it
This is a symbol of the new covenant

(Communion follows as music continues to play)

Peace, life, love is ours
Forgiveness, future, grace is ours
Faith, hope, peace is ours

Go in peace
God is alive
God is about us
Evermore

Roddy Hamilton 1996

Reflection

Be gentle when you touch bread,
Let it not lie uncared for – unwanted
So often bread is taken for granted
There is so much beauty in bread –
Beauty of sun and soil
Beauty of patient toil
Winds and rains have caressed it,
Christ often blest it.
Be gentle when you touch bread.

Be loving when you drink wine,
So freely received and joyfully shared
in the spirit of Him who cared,
Warm as a flowing river,
shining and clear as the sun,
Deep as the soil
of human toil,
The winds and the air caressed it,
Christ often blest it,
Be loving when you drink wine.

from Pilgrimage *by Ivor Smith-Cameron* 1987

Easter

Affirmation of faith

A celebration of what Easter is about: being the people of the Kingdom who know what it is to have said 'YES!' to life.

Leader   Today we have stood at the morning of
          the kingdom
       and we have glimpsed the future:
       and we have seen death's greatest failure
       and love's greatest triumph!
       We are the people of the kingdom!

All   *Alleluia! Christ is risen!*

Leader   Today we have seen the stone rolled away
       and witnessed the door of life open up.
       We have seen why there is hope in despair
       for we are caught in love's eternal brightness.
       We are the people of the kingdom!

All   *Alleluia! Christ is risen!*

Leader   Today we have talked to the gardener
       and seen the face of the risen Lord.
       We have witnessed just how God's promises
          are fulfilled,
       for we are now living on this side of the
          resurrection.
       We are the people of the kingdom!

All   *Alleluia! Christ is risen!*

Leader   Today we have stood with all the disciples
       of every time and place
       and looked into a tomb that is empty:
       We are taking part in the Good News of
          resurrection,
       for we have touched the joy that changes life
          into freedom;
       the hope that turns dreams into living;

the love that gathers together and rebuilds
  all the brokenness,
  all the lifelessness,
  all the longing
of yesterday's living
in today's amazing 'YES!' to life.
We are the people of the kingdom!

All   *Alleluia! Christ is risen!*

Roddy Hamilton 1997

Resurrection

In the beginning, a garden
where God and man
strolled in the scented twilight –
till the night began.

In the fullness of time in a garden
the Kingdom began
with sunrise, a weeping woman,
and a risen man.

But he, the lord of the garden,
is still betrayed
by those he trusted to cherish
the glory he made.

Unthinking, we seized on his bounty,
giving nothing back,
and made of his garden a desert
of ruin and wrack.

Oh, master gardener, hear us –
hear and forgive
our greed, our pride, our presumption;
teach us to live
in simplicity, charity, prudence,
guarding the earth,
tending your derelict garden
to joyful re-birth.

So when you shall come in splendour
to reprove and bless,
you may find us at work in a garden –
not a wilderness.

Peggy Day 1994

The gardener

Her face was turned from me,
Buried in her hands. Her loose cloak
Fluttered in the breeze
That carried the sound of her grieving
To where, amongst the olive trees,
I worked alone. 'Poor girl,' I thought,
'Come here to mourn a brother or a lover,
Soon to lie in the empty tomb
That stands close by.'
I didn't see the man
Until he called to her across the garden.
'A strange question,' I thought,
"Who are you looking for?"
Yet it seemed he had guessed aright –
She was searching, for the body
Of the man she mourned.
No wonder, then, at her distress –
Not a death only, but a disappearance.

My own eyes blurred at such intensity
Of pain, and I was turning, to avoid her grief,
When he spoke again –
A single word, so soft I couldn't catch it,
Yet she heard:
I saw her wheel round, saw her face
Transformed by sudden overwhelming joy,
You would have thought, to see her,
Her brother or her lover had returned.

Margaret Crawshaw 1996

Easter prayer

*This might effectively be spoken by a variety
of different voices.*

May the risen Christ who called Mary by her name
    come to you to reassure you
    that he knows you and loves you as if there
      was no one else.

May the risen Christ who walked with his friends
    all the way to Emmaus, interpreting the scriptures
      for them,
    come to you to guide you in your pilgrimage
    and to lead you into truth.

May the risen Christ who sat down at the supper table
    and broke the bread
    come to you to bless you at your tables;
    and may he come to us all, gathered at his table,
    to feed us with the Bread of Life.

May the risen Christ who breathed his peace on his disciples
    come to you to give you peace
    in the assurance of his forgiveness,
    that you may be a channel of his peace in
    and for a troubled world.

May the risen Christ who showed his wounds to his disciples
    come to you to give you that healing of your wounds
    which will be for the strengthening of your life with him
    and to the glory of his name.

May the risen Christ who met Thomas in his doubting
    come to you to give you the happiness he promised
    to those who have never seen him and yet believe.

May the risen Christ who prepared breakfast for his friends
    while they fished on the lake
    come to you in your places of work

to help you honour God and serve your neighbour in all
    you do there.

May the risen Christ who sent his apostles to make
    disciples of all the nations
    come to you to strengthen you in your witness to him
    day by day.

May the risen Christ who has gone ahead of us
    to prepare a place for us
    come to you at the hour of your death
    to take you to your eternal home.

The Lord bless you as you keep the Easter season
    and fill you with his life and his love,
    for your own sake, in the service of others,
    and above all to his everlasting glory.

David Flynn 1992

Bus to Emmaus

Sorry, I didn't see you standing there.
No, no one's seat.
A full bus, isn't it.
Excuse me, don't I know you? . . . at the church?
Quite often: yes, I felt sure, but can't quite . . .
No, I've not been there lately. Not at all.
Not even Easter Sunday, I'm afraid.

Evenings like these are Easter now for me,
A cold clear sky above the silent hills,
and the lambs crying.

We never even knew that she was ill,
our little girl, until it was too late,
an empty mask and not her face at all.
Doctor said, Sorry, I'm afraid she's dead.
Always we're sorry, always we're afraid.
The curate called, I have to give him that,
and then he said, It's God's will. Jim stood up,
and said, Get out of my house.
Jim's very bitter.
Do **you** think it was God's will?

If you're a man for healing, as you say,
God's will for you is only in the cures,
and not the illness or the dying part,
I quite see that. Is **that** what Scripture says?
The Lord did nothing but the Will of God
and never hurt a soul?
Healing and peace
speak, oh, a voice like music to the world.

But the world seems all parting and all pain.

What did those women really know that day?
Could they say honestly, I've been beyond
the locked gate, been behind the mirror,
and there was dew and brightness in a garden?

God knows how much I want it to be true.
Wanting can't make a truth, can it? Or tears.

Here comes the village, and my journey's end.
Thank you for letting me say what I feel.
My heart was burning in me on the way.
You understood that.
This stop, driver.
See,
that light shines in our kitchen, through the dusk.
Why not come in and have a cup of tea?
It takes no time at all to boil a kettle.

Brenda Jackson 1997

This is my . . .

This is my Body –
So you tell us, Jesus;
My Body
strong and active,
clothed and fed,
Unfit for death.

This is my Body –
So you tell us, Jesus;
My Blood
My life
Outpoured upon a cross
by cruel hands
– in love.

Body of Jesus –
Be present
in your world;
Let bound and broken
starved and homeless
touch you.

Blood of Jesus –
Be life to
drained and weary
sick and dying.

And in your Sacrament of
Body and of Blood
Forgive and cleanse,
Revive, Restore
your waning Church,
And be through us,
the world's undying hope.

David M. Owen 1989

Before the Easter icon

'He descended into hell . . .
the third day He rose again from the dead . . .'

Rise Up! Lord of the Living
    from the grave,
    and come to us
    the longing and the long forgotten,
    and break the claim of death
    that we may rise
    with You
    with joy . . .
    Alleluia!

Rise Up! Lord Christ
    from death and all decay,
    and bring us with You from the tomb
    in all Your splendour . . .
    Alleluia!

Rise Up! the sad, the mourners,
    the broken and the sick at heart;
    your hope He now brings with Him . . .
    Alleluia!

Rise Up! the faithful, and the doubting
    still unsure,
    to the New Day
    to share its light
    in which we recognise
    It is the Lord!
    Alleluia!

Rise Up! creation now new-dressed
    from shrouds of cold,
    and with us
    find new voice to praise Him
    who makes all things new
    in this New Thing . . .
    Alleluia!

Rise Up! within us, Lord,
    your living Body,
    and from worn sins
    and old archaic ways
    deliver us;
    sing in us the New Song
    Alleluia!

Kenneth Carveley 1989

Nine seasonal collects

Easter (Matthew 28.1-10)

God of terror and joy,
you arise to shake the earth;
open our graves
and give us back the past;
so that all that has been buried
may be freed and forgiven,
and our lives may return to you
    through the risen Christ.

Easter 1 (John 20.19-21)

Risen Christ,
whose absence leaves us paralysed,
but whose presence is overwhelming,
breathe on us
with your abundant life;
that where we cannot see
we may have courage to believe
that we may be raised with you.

Easter 2 (Luke 22.13-35)

O God whose greeting we miss
and whose departure we cannot bear,
make our hearts burn with insight
on our ordinary road;
that, as we grasp you in the broken bread,
we may also let you go,
and return to speak your word of life
    in the name of Christ.

Julian's Day (8 May)

Christ our true Mother,
you have carried us within you,
laboured with us,
and brought us forth to bliss.
Enclose us in your care,
that in stumbling we may not fall,
nor be overcome by evil,
but know that all shall be well.

Easter 3 (John 11.17-27)

O God, you call us to commitment
even at the point of despair.
Give us the faith of Martha
to find in our anger and loss
a truthful place to proclaim you
our resurrection and life,
      through Jesus Christ.

Easter 4 (John 21.15-22)

Christ our friend,
you ask for our love
in spite of our betrayal.
Give us courage to embrace forgiveness,
know you again,
and trust ourselves in you.

Easter 5 (John 16.12-24)

O God for whom we long
as a woman in labour
longs for her delivery;
give us courage to wait,
strength to push,
and discernment to know the right time;
that we may bring into the world
your joyful peace,
      through Jesus Christ.

Visitation (31 May)

O God our deliverer,
you cast down the mighty,
and lift up those of no account;
as Elizabeth and Mary embraced
with songs of liberation,
so may we be pregnant with your Spirit,
and affirm one another in hope for the world,
     through Jesus Christ.

Ascension Day

O God,
you withdraw from our sight
that you may be known by our love:
help us to enter the cloud
where you are hidden,
and surrender all our certainty
to the darkness of faith
     in Jesus Christ.

Suzanne Fageol 1989

But nobody went to his burial

This was written for the Sunday after Ascension, responding to Luke's account of Judas' demise but reminding the congregation of the Matthew tradition of his suicide. It was a response to a number in the congregation who were facing crises in their personal faith. It followed the Scripture Reading, Acts 1.12-26.

He had let the rest down.

> No one came near him. Loyalty exacts a high price when you have to question yours.

He had his reasons.

> But no one came near him. He had no chance to explain. Although he wanted to, he struggled to find the words. The deed proclaimed his isolation and nothing was done to change that.

He felt alone, ignored, discarded.

> For no one came near him. There is no more hurtful vengeance than the silence of those to whom you once belonged.

He was on his own, self-accusing, self-absorbed.

> And no one came near him.

The news of his death spread, whispered with knowing looks and self-righteous tone. The body was disposed of quickly. There is no record of any fellow disciple at his burial, not even standing at a distance.

They did not know what to say. They were hurt beyond words. Nothing could take away what had been done.

So they turned to the future. Some searched among the

scriptures for a 'word' to settle it but:

> He was a threat.
> He had broken ranks.
> They had known he wouldn't fit in.
> He had come from another place.
> His accent, his background and now his mercenary
>   act of folly said it all.

He was different.
A barrier too great for them to climb.

'Judas!'

'Lord?'

'Didn't you think we would meet again? You knew we were both victims of God's fate; though in the future they will call that Providence. Can you give me another chance?'

'Lord?'

'They'll say in the future you failed me. But was that really the case? Let me try again, Judas. After all, I have been through a lot more. Look, the scars prove it!'

Let us pray:

Eternal God,

Forgive us when we place others in isolation because what they say or won't say or believe or do reminds us of our own frailty and incompleteness.

Forgive us when we burden those who feel failures with words meant kindly but which just fend off the issue.

Help us to be a church that is as welcoming to people with their questions, mistakes, resentment as we are when they look as if they will be no trouble.

Help us to confess our disillusionment, fears and flaws so that pretence is kept to a minimum and we are a community based on honesty.

In the name of One who never turned away from another person, even when he had betrayal in his eye, the living Saviour, Jesus Christ our Lord.

John Rackley 1996

Become our resurrection

Living God
save us
from confining your activity
to the distant past
and the far off future.

Give us the courage
    to expect your action
    in the world as it is
    as you bring new life to birth
    before our eyes.

Give us the vigilance
    to watch for the movement
    of your spirit
    in the tumult of nations
    and the voices of nature
    in the cultures which are strange to us
    and in the religious traditions
    which we find hard to understand.

Give us the vision
    to sense your hand upon our future
    as we come to terms
    with changing patterns of work and leisure,
    as we discover new truths about the universe,
    and as we explore the beginning and end
    of human existence.

Living Jesus
become for us
the Resurrection
each day
as we seek to live
gloriously
and responsibly
by your love.

David Jenkins 1997

A psalm of Falling and Rising

God of the Falling and of the Rising,
    do not give up on me.
Teach me to let my failings fall
    that I might rise to you.

Like a tree, clinging to its leaves
    when all around stand bare:
I cling to my failures,
    even when others have forgotten,
    or forgiven.
I cling to my pain,
    even though it holds me back
    from starting new growth.

Your breath would melt the frost on my heart,
    your desire is Springtime
To fill my heart,
    my life,
    my community.

Release me from the dead leaves
    of expectations
Bring forth buds
    of hope,
    the leaves which are for healing

As the sap is withdrawn
    to wither the leaves,
If your love were withdrawn from me
    I would wither and perish.

Preserve me then,
    through the Winter of Guilt,
    through the gales of conflict.
That I might stand at last,
    resplendent with the foliage of your Word.

Falling, may I be held,
    to rise with the Springtime Son.

Allan R. Smith 1995

Christ the healer

Lord Jesus Christ, who endured
    the violence of mocking and verbal abuse,
Heal and comfort children the world over,
    whose lives are warped by words which
    scar their minds;
Heal and comfort children, women and men
    who are the victims of racial abuse;
Heal and comfort all those
    whose homosexuality is the butt of humour,
    the target of abuse,
    the object of legislation,
so that they cannot be free to be
    the selves that God created them to be.

Lord Jesus Christ, who endured
    the violence of the scourge,
Heal and comfort children, women and men
    who are beaten
    tortured
    physically abused
    by the violence of others.

Lord Jesus Christ, who endured
    the violence of the rejection of friends,
Heal and comfort children, women and men
    whose lives are misshapen by
    lovelessness
    rejection
    broken trust;
Heal and support those who are imprisoned,
    detained, kidnapped, and so feel the
    loneliness of separation from those they love.

Lord Jesus Christ, who endured
    the violence of the cross,
Heal and comfort all who die
    on the cross of hunger, disease and poverty
    so that others may live in health and plenty;

Heal and comfort all who die
    on the cross of injustice
    false witness
    racism
    and intolerance.

Lord Jesus Christ, who endured
    the cross, despising the shame and have now
    taken your seat beside God,
Heal and comfort us in our own need,
    our loved ones in their need,
    and all for whom we are asked to pray today.

Hugh Cross 1989

Pentecost and the life of the Church

A litany of thanksgiving

Remember them
    they mark the way of faith;
people of prayer and perception
of clear faith and humility
obedient and trusting,

for the grace we find in them
the God of grace be praised.

Remember them
    they point the way to truth;
patriarchs, prophets,
apostles, evangelists,
preachers,
teachers of wisdom,
in season and out of season,
to listening or unheeding,

for the truth we know through them
the God of truth be praised.

Remember them
    compassionate and caring;
pastors, intercessors,
advocates, visitors,
servants, and ministers to need,
supporting, encouraging and consoling,

for the love revealed in them
the God of love be praised.

Remember them
    faithful, in doubt and uncertainty;
persecuted, martyrs,
confessors, unknown,
imprisoned, tortured,
never forsaken,
sharing the suffering of our Lord's Body,

for the strength we see in them
the mighty God be praised.

Remember them
    they see God's possibilities;
visionaries and dreamers,
mystics and contemplatives,
desiring better and patiently waiting.
Glimpsing the future
through present darkness,

for the hope we share with them
the God of hope be praised.

Remember them
    reconcilers and healers;
who cross divides
bind up broken hearts,
proclaim release for captives,
give understanding,

for the peace we seek with them
the God of peace be praised.

Remember them
    living and departed;
on earth and in heaven
One family
One people
One joy
One song

for our life in Christ with them
the living God be praised.

Kenneth Carveley 1988

Who travelled to follow Christ's Way

We praise you, God,
for those who have travelled abroad
    not to see sights,
    not to exploit,
    not only to solve problems,
    not only to share their own strengths,
but to live and to identify,
and there to learn
what it means to follow Christ's Way,
and to invite others to join them in it.

For journeys taken out of love,
for contacts made in humility,
and for hearts ready to enfold the new,
the strange and the alarming,
we praise you.

For the modern missionary movement,
and your use of it, Lord,
enriching visitor and visited,
senders and sent,
rich and poor,
we give thanks in the name of Jesus.

Stuart Jenkins 1992

A meditation on a storm

I'd never heard a real
    'rushing mighty wind'
        till last October.
Then suddenly – and was it sudden! –
I woke up, and there it was.
But not just 'there', it was everywhere,
    shouting with urgency,
        irresistible in its pressure,
            awe-inspiring in its power.
It was moving faster than comprehension
and most things moved with it.

In the morning, look!
    devastation and disorder,
        mourning for trees and damage,
            silence on the telephone,
silence in the roads,
    – no one can get through –
        ways are blocked.

Are you all right?
    did it come your way?
        is the family safe?
            it's just like the blitz!
    a catastrophe!
    Things will never be the same again,
        a lifetime's work blown down . . .
And they say something rather like it
    is happening on the Stock Exchange.
God shouldn't allow things like this.

But I seem to remember,
    talking about God,
        wasn't there once an event
            which was rather similar?
People said it was the start
    of the Christian Church!
        Heavens, yes!

when God showed up in a rushing
mighty wind!

Thank God it blew at night
so very few were hurt:
and we looked at each other properly
and, for once, helped our
neighbours.

The lovely old tree in our garden
has gone, and fences with it:
but there's much more light now.

Daphne Fraser 1988

Holy Spirit come

Holy Spirit come
Inspire our praying,
That we may touch your life in God
Beyond our saying.

Holy Spirit come
Inform our knowing,
That we may follow after truth
Beyond our showing.

Holy Spirit come
Enrich our meeting,
That we may others now include
Beyond our greeting.

Holy Spirit come
Direct our living,
That we may share a daily grace
Beyond our giving.

Holy Spirit come
Comfort our sighing,
That we may hope for life renewed
Beyond our dying.

Geoffrey Ainger 1991

Love, truth and openness

There are things
that I can't talk to him about
because, if I did,
he might feel that I am not the person
he thought I was.

There are things
that he can't talk to me about
because, he thinks that if he did,
I might feel that he is not the person
I thought him to be.

Because I can't talk to him
about these things
that I can't talk to him about,
I behave differently
and no doubt
he is wondering why I've changed.
This is one of the things
he would like to talk about with me.

Because he can't talk to me
about these things
that he can't talk to me about,
he behaves differently
and I wonder why he has changed.
This is one of the things
I would like to talk about with him.

Society likes to preserve the façade;
to pretend that nothing has changed
and therefore,
that we have nothing to talk about
that we might find ourselves
unable to talk about.

It encourages us to pretend
and not to say
what is in our hearts to say,
when we talk.
The Enemy would have us
become strangers to one another again;
as if the Spirit had not moved
over the face of the waters
to bring order out of chaos.

How important it is
that love should mean openness
and that we should be able
to speak truly to one another.

Alastair Dykes 1994

Prayer rosary

Hiroshima,
Bosnia,
Belfast,
the names slip through our fingers,
like blood-stained beads.

As we tell the story,
tell us,
tell us,
tell us,
the way
to peace.

Beirut,
Nagasaki,
Nuremberg,
Still they come,
Countless numbers:
people hounded,
refugees tramping the road
out of hell, into hell.

Where will it stop?
Show us,
show us,
show us,
the way to peace.

Five for sorrow,
ten for joy,
may what has been sown in pain
be reaped in hope.

Kate McIlhagga 1994

Disciple

I will follow you.

I will go to the ends of the earth for you
so long as the earth is round.

I will die to the flesh
in the sure and certain hope of resurrection.

I will put away the old man
for safe keeping.

Your yoke is easy –
that's good.
I don't mind what it costs
if I can afford it.

I don't mind doing my bit on the cross.
We could have a rota.
Put me down for a couple of hours
Sunday evening

and please don't use nails.

I will follow you
carefully,
with helpful advice.

I will follow you
wherever I want to go.

Godfrey Rust 1992

Help us to admit our emptiness

Prayer based on the story of the Prodigal

Spirit hovering over our chaos,
help us to acknowledge our sin;
lead us to deeper repentance in unity with Christ.
Help us to admit our emptiness
that we may turn to be filled
with the love that rushes to meet us.
May we be more conscious of God's goodness
than of our own guilt.

May we allow ourselves to be embraced and kissed
by the Father, who delights in us,
and if we look out of the eyes of the other,
the elder brother, in jealousy and pain,
help us to admit our emptiness
that we may turn to be filled
with the love that says:
my son, my daughter,
you are with me always
and all I have is yours.

When we see the happiness of Father and children
through the smoke of the cooking fire,
from behind the daily juggling act of unfinished tasks,
may our tears be ones of joy,
as we admit our emptiness,
our longing for fulfilment
and receive the understanding love
which empowers and enables us
to serve by being ourselves.

Kate McIlhagga 1992

Authority from being sufferers with Christ

Let us pray for those who have authority
because they suffer with Christ.
Those who are weak, abused, broken or rejected.
Sisters and brothers of Christ,
whose authority comes from their experience of crucifixion.

May we catch a glimpse of their Christ-likeness,
and submit ourselves to their God-given authority,
by serving them, and being befriended by them.

So may we be healed of our fear of those who suffer,
and may those who suffer in this way
be reassured of their worth,
as we name Christ in them.

> Lord hear us.
> Lord, graciously hear us.

Jonathan Martin 1990

A Laodicean estate agent writes

The developers have moved in
on 1 Corinthians 13
(a delightful period chapter
retaining many of the original features)

The structural survey found
Faith, Hope and Love
inadequate for modern requirements

The valuers found
that it profited them nothing

The planning office saw
as in a glass, darkly

The architect
believed all things

The contractor
hoped all things

The neighbours
endured all things

The builders
spoke with the tongues of men
and definitely not angels

and now it's done and back on the market
these three remain
Ambition, Fear and Need

and the greatest of these
is never satisfied.

Godfrey Rust 1991

On the edge

Living on the edge of the church
I am tolerated
patronized or even pitied
because I haven't seen the Light
and can't accept the Truth
of its teaching or tradition.

But the light can be a fire of love
or the blinding glare of a torture chamber.
The light of the church
has been both
is both.
So I must choose
when to add my candle to that light.

And truth can be a liberation
or an imprisoning strait-jacket.
The truth of the church
has been both
is both.
So I must choose
when to add my candle to that truth.

Living on the edge of the church
my candle is unseen
the whisper of my truth unheard.
If my candle joins the others
to make a warmer glow
the church turns its face away.
If my whisper becomes a shout
the church closes its ears.
Are my light and truth
so frightening
that they must be rejected out of hand?
Are my questions so threatening
that they can't be entertained
for a moment?
Is the church so blind and deaf

that it can only see its own art
hear only its own music?
How many bonfires must I light
how many megaphones must I use?

Living on the edge of the church
is dangerous
for bonfires can rage
out of control
and megaphones deafen
or seem to blow my own trumpet.

Yet the light of truth
is a candle
which with other candles
dispels the dark
without destroying it.
And the whisper of truth
arises from the depths of wisdom
and is easy to miss
in the din of shouting.

If I can't make myself
seen or heard
without a raging fire
or a deafening shout
I risk destroying
what truth I have.

Living on the edge of the church
is dangerous
for if I draw near to the church
and my light is not seen
and my truth not heard
I risk being absorbed
and buried with my truth
within the system of the church.
Then my candle no longer lights my way
and the whisper of my wisdom
no longer guides my step

Living on the edge of the church
is lonely.
It would be easier
to surrender my mind
to its teaching and tradition.
I would then be accepted
and welcomed as a true son.
I want to be accepted
but I cannot live a lie.
I can only stand on the edge
until my whispering wisdom
can make itself heard
within the church.
Maybe the church will learn
to listen.
Maybe I shall learn
to speak
in a more penetrating whisper.
Until then I must live my truth on the edge.

Peter Brice 1993
(*From* Trust *No.4, Sept. 1991, SCM Press*)

Belonging: children's meditations and prayers

Rejection is what I face when I walk into the classroom.
Attacks are what I fear when I leave at the end of the day.
Calling names and spitting at me, like I'm some sort of animal.
I try to ignore their lashing tongues, don't they see I'm just
another colour?
Sometimes I cry when I know what I have to face.
Matters of life and death because of a different colour . . . a
different race.

Dear Lord,
We pray for all those children who have lost their families
either through splitting up or death. I pray that one day they
may have a family of their own and will forget about their
loneliness as a child, and they will also belong to a family,
a family of their own and that they will learn to love and
care for it and to get on with their lives.

Dear God,
Everyone wants to belong, whether it's to a group, family or
community. Sometimes we exclude people from the groups
we belong to, just because we don't see people for who they
really are, just what's on the outside. Please help us to be more
welcoming to others, making them feel they belong. Amen.

Dear Lord,
As I look around the world today, all I see is sadness. People
think I don't belong, because I'm not the same, but I don't
want to be the same. I want to be me. I'm who I am not who
everyone wants me to be. I'm me and I'm proud of it, because
I'm me.
Lord, hear us.

Dear Lord,
Why oh why don't I belong
Is it me, is there something wrong?
Why am I so hard to like

And people tell me to take a hike.
I don't understand,
I am so confused
I'm cold and alone, I feel abused
Everything changes but me.
I'm a thousand miles apart and
        no one loves me.
Lord I don't know what to do.
Please help me to see this through.
I have faith, I won't give up hope,
But I don't know how long I can cope.
You're always there
You know how I feel
Please help me Lord
I know you will.

Personal prayers on the theme 'Belonging'
written by students of Gumley House School,
Isleworth, Hounslow 1995

A question of language

God, why is it so much of our Christianity
seems to be for grown-ups only?
You know quite well most of us
don't talk theology all day long
and certainly not
all through our church services
(think of some of our hymns!).
But our language goes elaborate
and pompous, when You're mentioned.
No need for this at all –
or why the incarnation?
Jesus was born a baby –
had to learn to speak, to grow up;
then when he spoke, he talked in parables
in symbols, in analogies . . .
Mustard seeds, lost coins,
camels and needles, specks of sawdust . . .
and a child could understand him.
And children liked him,
and he liked children.
As children grow, they learn to speak:
so why can't we use language properly –
for the children we still are
and the grown-ups we become?

Daphne Fraser 1995

A prayer for the parish

Disturb us, Lord, when we are too well
    pleased with ourselves,
When our dreams have come true because we
    dreamed too little,
When we arrive safely because we sailed too
    close to the shore.

Disturb us, Lord, when with the abundance
    of things we possess,
We have lost our thirst for the waters of life;
Having fallen in love with life, we have
    ceased to dream of eternity,
And in our efforts to build a new earth,
We have allowed our vision of the new
    Heaven to dim.

Disturb us, Lord, to dare more boldly,
To venture on wider seas, where storms will
    show your mastery;
Where losing sight of land, we shall find
    the stars.
We ask you to push back the horizons of
    our hopes,
And to push us in the future in strength,
    courage, hope, and love.

This we ask in the name of our Captain, who
    is Jesus Christ.

St James' Church, New York City 1995
(*from* The Anglican Digest)

The healing of laughter

Teach me to laugh, Lord,
Show me what to laugh about –
Not the hypocrisy of sly digs and spiteful mockery
But the healthy chortle, like the chuckle of a child
That bubbles up from within from sheer delight.

I can remember that feeling, Lord,
Though I can't remember how, or when, or where.
I can remember the laughter welling up unbidden
And the uncontrollable, infectious chuckle
As a child, and later as a young adult.

Lord, I seem to have become so earnest these days.
A quiet smile is all I allow myself to reveal,
So that, when I do laugh, really laugh,
it takes me by surprise.

What has happened to the effervescent joy
that used to spill over
Through everything, on all occasions,
to all people?

Lord, teach me how to laugh again
Show me how to laugh at myself!

Mary Teed 1995

Send your Holy Spirit

Leader   Living Lord,
send your Holy Spirit
like wind to waken your church,
like fire to enflame your people with
    living hope,

Response   *Come, wind and fire of the Spirit,*
    enflame us forever with the passion of
    Christ's love.

Leader   Living Lord,
send your Holy Spirit
like wind to stir your world,
like fire to renew the earth.

Response   *Come, wind and fire of the Spirit,*
    enflame us forever with the passion of
    Christ's love.

Leader   Living Lord,
send your Holy Spirit
like wind to enliven this community,
like fire to warm our common life.

Response   *Come, wind and fire of the Spirit,*
    enflame us forever with the passion of
    Christ's love.

Leader   Living Lord,
send your Holy Spirit
like wind to soothe the wounds
    of the sick,
like fire to cleanse the minds
    of the tormented.

Response   *Come, wind and fire of the Spirit,*
    enflame us forever with the passion of
    Christ's love.

Leader   Living Lord,
               send your Holy Spirit
               like wind to rouse up the witness of
                   your saints,
               like fire to inscribe the testimony of
                   their lives in our hearts.

Response   *Come, wind and fire of the Spirit,*
                   enflame us forever with the passion of
                   Christ's love.

                                   Nicola Slee 1989

Thank you for your presence with us

Dear God
thank you for your presence with us
searching us out
in the deep places of our lives
and leading us on
to new understandings
of your will and purpose
for the world you have made and love

thank you for resurrection hope
        and pentecostal power
which enable us to make new beginnings
and find the strength and courage
to go on our pilgrim way,
so that despair gives way to hope,
        hatred to love,
        and violence to peace
in our lives, our communities and our world

thank you for Jesus
risen, ascended, glorified,
to be embodied in us
in whose name and for whose sake we come.

Betty Hares 1989

Harvest

Heard at Harvest

'The nights are closing in,
stubble burnt, leaves burning,
logs waiting in the hearth,
the great wheel turning.
I'm cold.'
The year is old.

'All Christian feasts are feasts of the happy ending,
star out of dark stable, sun out of dark tomb,
and what end is happy that does not begin?
Light up the church, then, in these dwindling days,
with faith and hope in one great golden blaze.'

Mist fills the croft.
'Close the barn door
on the last load.
Shut up the apples in the loft.
our harvest praise
is sung.'

Deep in dark earth,
the year is young.

Brenda Jackson 1996

The dandelion

Like a dandelion my faith grows and flourishes in the cracks
and crevices of life, taking root in the most unlikely of places.

My faith is firm and full of life, sunny, just as the flower of the
dandelion is full of life and bright yellow.

But then, just when everything is comfortable and serene,
something happens. It is as though the world that is so
safe and secure becomes fragile, just like the clock of the
dandelion, fragile and so delicate that the slightest movement
will send the pieces flying away.

My faith from being securely rooted is disturbed. I find it hard
to see God's hand at work. I cry to Him, but cannot see what is
happening and I become stripped of all I am, bereft, just as the
stalk of the dandelion is stripped of its head. I forget that the
stalk is still rooted in the ground being fed by the leaves, all I
know is that my faith which seemed so strong is so no longer.

It is then, when I am nothing, that God in His infinite
mercy comes and fills me, touching me with His love,
His compassion, His strength, His life. It is then I realise the
seeds that blew away and left me bare, have in fact rooted
themselves deep within me, and the faith I thought had gone
has become stronger because of the experience of being
emptied and filled anew.

I don't like the times when I feel so insecure, when it seems
my faith is fickle, yet I now know that through these times
I am being brought back to God in a deeper relationship
which helps me to grow, and I need the barren times in order
to appreciate the harvest, otherwise I take God for granted.

I thank God for the dandelions in my life that help me to see
God more clearly.

Denise Creed 1996

Work is love made visible

Work is love made visible
  if you cannot work with love but only
    with distaste,
it is better that you should leave your work
  and sit at the gate
of the temple and take alms of those who
  work with joy.

Work is love made visible
  if you bake bread with indifference, you
    bake a bitter bread
that feeds but half human hunger.

Work is love made visible
  if you grudge the crushing of the grapes,
    your grudge distils a poison
in the wine.

Work is love made visible
  if you sing though as angels, and love
    not the singing,
you muffle our ears to the voices of the day
  and the voices of the night.

Work is love made visible
Lord, send us to live and work to your praise
  and glory,
so that we and all your family may enter upon
  the liberty and splendour of
the children of God.

Author unknown 1990

A dancer

A Christian must be like a dancer.
>Every tendon and muscle of her belief must
>be
>>flexible, supple, yet strong.
She must keep time to the music of Christ's
word,
>making her movements
>>natural and confident.

Like the dancer the Christian cannot limit her
dance
>to one aspect of her life,
>>But must cover the whole of the stage.
Her imagination and dedication must equal that
of
>the dancer, ever trying to find new forms of
>>expressing her art,
>>>searching and exploring,
pushing back the boundaries of her capabilities,
>falling, rising again, determined to
>continue
>>the dance
>>>until it is perfected.

The Christian must have the dancer's courage
and
>be ready to rise to that great occasion and
>>to accept the gracious applause of
>>>God's love.

Weoley Castle Community Church 1987

Three farmers

a harvest story . . .

Resources: 3 packets of seeds,
 umbrella, blue cloth,
 sun picture,
 cereal packets.
 Labels; Names. Areas

Farmers: John *in England*
 Elizabeth *in Africa*
 Raj *in Asia*

*The story is about three farmers in different circumstances.
It ends with a question for the congregation. This story
requires three 'volunteers' to be the farmers. They have
no spoken part, and so can be enacted by children, or
adults, with minimal preparation.*

*The narrator reads the story and can also 'manage' props.
During the story the props are introduced as indicated
(words in italics).*

*The farmers stand at the front – with their name badges
and places to 'set the scene'.*

One year three farmers prepared their land.
John ploughed the fields with his tractor,
Elizabeth dug and worked her shamba* with a jembe,*
Raj prepared his fields with an oxen-powered plough.
	(*farmers prepare the land*)
All three farmers worked hard, and their soil was soon ready
for planting.
	(*give each farmer a packet of seeds*)
John sowed his fields with wheat,
	(*he sows the seeds*)
Elizabeth sowed her shamba with maize,
	(*she sows the seeds*)
and Raj planted cereal in his fields.
	(*he sows the seeds*)

Each farmer knew that they had to grow enough food to take
to the market, or to a big company, to sell so that they would
be able to support their family that year.

John, Elizabeth and Raj worked hard.
They all tended their young crops,
and looked forward to the harvest.

It was the time for the rain to come, and help the young
seedlings to grow into strong plants.

In May the rain came in England. There was not as much rain
that summer as in previous years, but there was enough. The
plants grew well.

The rain came too in the part of Asia where Raj and his family
lived (*umbrella*). It came, and kept coming, and the fields were
flooded and the crop was ruined (*blue cloth = flood*).

The rain did not come to Elizabeth's part of Africa this year (*sun*).
Elizabeth tried to irrigate the plants, but the water supply was
not reliable or sufficient. The land became drier and drier, the
wind swept the soil into fine dust and the crops dried up and
died in the drought.

Then came the harvest time.
John worked hard throughout the summer days and evenings . . .
and harvested a sufficient crop of wheat.
It had not been easy, and there were lots of problems, but there
was a harvest.
   (*he collects all the cereal packets*)

Raj tried to save what he could, but there was little he
could do.
He had to borrow money to start again, so now he was also
in debt.

Elizabeth continued to work at trying to coax the dried out ground into growing some food, but it was difficult, she and the family were always hungry, and she needed a more reliable source of water.

(FREEZE. *All the farmers freeze in position, John with his harvest – Elizabeth and Raj still trying to work)*

And that was the end of the story . . .
Or is it?

The response of those watching varies from protest, declaring that John must share his produce (symbolic of our situation) to – 'yes, that is the end of the story.' Both responses provide a starting point for looking at **our own** *response and responsibility.*

> *'shamba'= allotment*
> *'jembe'= digging tool (like a huge hoe)*

Morag Walder 1994

Help us to be true to our calling

Lord, we thank you that you have called us
    to be your people:
    to offer you our worship;
    to be a living fellowship;
    to be a serving people.

        Lord, on this our day of dedication:
        Help us to be true to our calling.

Help us, Lord,
    to offer worship that is true and honest;
    the worship of heart and mind and spirit;
    offering to you
    the best of the gifts you have given.

        Lord, on this our day of dedication:
        Help us to be true to our calling.

Help us, Lord,
    to offer a loving community;
    a community where each one feels at home;
    each person finds a place,
    able to give and to receive,
    offering to each other
    the best of the gifts you have given.

        Lord, on this our day of dedication:
        Help us to be true to our calling.

Help us, Lord,
>to offer service that is courageous and humble;
>the service of your love to us;
>that by the way we give
>all may know your loving care;
>offering to people everywhere
>the best of the gifts you have given.

>>Lord, on this our day of dedication:
>>*Help us to be true to our calling.*

>>>>>*David Blanchflower* 1989

Credo from Nicaragua

I believe in God, creator of an unfinished world,
who does not decree an eternal plan of development
in which we cannot participate.

I believe in God,
who has not divided people into the poor and rich,
specialists and the ignorant, owners and slaves.

I believe in Jesus Christ,
who saw the world situation and who took a stand in it.

Taking him as my example,
I see the precaution with which we must organize,
the extent to which our intelligence is atrophied,
our imagination impoverished, and our efforts neutralised.

Each day I fear that he may have died in vain
because we do not live as he lived,
because we betray his message.

I believe in Jesus Christ, who rises for our life,
so that we may be liberated
from the prejudices and presumptions of fear and hate,
so that we may transform the world into the Kingdom
        of God.

I believe in the Spirit who came with Jesus into the world.

I believe in the community of all peoples,
and in our responsibility
for making of our world a place of misery, hunger
        and violence,
or a City of God.

Anon. 1987
(from Nicaragua)

Before the harvest

'I appointed you to go on and bear fruit, fruit that will last'
(John 15.16, REB)

Before the harvest
the ripening,
before the ripening
the growing,
before the growing
the sowing,
before the sowing
the preparation of the soil.

May we be so prepared
for the Spirit's sowing
that the seed
may grow in fruitful soil
and ripen to a worthy harvest.

Edmund Banyard 1991

Agriculture and rural life

*The following was used at a weekend conference held in
Norwich to talk about agriculture and rural life from a Christian
perspective. You are invited to adapt it to your own situation.*

Let us picture the farms of East Anglia, the people who own
them, manage them and work on them. They know many joys
but also deep uncertainties:
Here in the world

All   Meet with your people Lord.

Life on the farm is affected by decisions made in London,
Brussels, Strasbourg and elsewhere. For parliaments and
officials, the making of good decisions is not easy:
Here in the world

All   Meet with your people Lord.

The countryside is being opened up for more and more leisure
and tourist activities, to the enjoyment of many people:
Here in the world

All   Meet with your people Lord.

Villages are becoming mixed communities of local people
and commuters with much to give to one another but
sometimes divided:
Here in the world

All   Meet with your people Lord.

Let us reflect upon the food chain and all the people who
grow, process, pack, transport, retail and serve food:
Here in the world

All   Meet with your people Lord.

For most of the people of this city, this lunchtime will bring
good food and much enjoyment of it:
Here in the world

All   Meet with your people Lord.

As we think of our own blessings, we remember the sufferings
of others
   where poor soil is made poorer by
   inappropriate technology
   where the local production of food is interfered with by
   powerful external sources
   where premature death is caused by hunger:
Here in the world

All   Meet with your people Lord.

We think of universities and colleges where young people
prepare themselves for lives in the farming and food industries
and for work and service in rural areas:
Here in the world

All   Meet with your people Lord.

We think of the people of the press, television and other media
who have much influence over how issues are seen and
understood:
Here in the world

All   Meet with your people Lord..

Creator God, we praise you that you are constantly at work
in your creation, that in Jesus you meet us joyfully and in
suffering love, that your Holy Spirit pervades the world and
that we can offer these prayers in confidence and trust, to the
glory of your name.

Michael Powell 1991

I ask for daily bread

I ask for daily bread,
but not for riches,
for fear of forgetting the poor.

I ask for strength,
but not for force,
for fear of disdaining the gentle.

I ask for wisdom,
but not for learning,
for fear of scorning the simple.

I ask that my name be honoured,
but not glorified,
for fear of crushing the humble.

I ask for a peaceful spirit,
but not for idle hours,
for fear of missing the call to serve.

Inazo Nitobe 1992

The web of creation

I live in a world
where air, trees, plants,
water and fire
creatures and lands
link to each other
for food, for life,
for balance, for use.
A world which was made
for them all – and for me.

God lives in a life
of holiness, joy,
of balance and truth,
of justice and peace
where Spirit links One
with the Others, in love.

God looked, and God said,
Let us make! Let us make!
So God spun the whole universe
from atom to galaxy
in the web of his love.
It was great, it was good,
there was meaning for all.
God even provided
true meaning for me.

But the story went on:
there was trouble for earth;
for we humans did not
get the drift of God's plan.
The web tattered and tore –
lost were justice and peace.

So God moved in again
and at fearful expense
made a way to restore
the great tangle we'd made.

So I live in a world
where the lines of the web
in and out of our mess,
out and in to God's love
co-exist for a time.
Praise to God for the web,
for the way to re-plan,
for the chance for us, too
to create;
to make
Love.

Daphne Fraser 1990

White powder

I saw the pain in your faces
as you heard the story
of bauxite extraction in Jamaica,
a white landscape ripped apart
with excavators,
a great wind blowing vast quantities
of white powder-dust into houses,
bringing fears of lasting damage
to lungs and health.

I see the perplexity on your faces
as you ask what you my people,
can do about such things
as terrifying snow-storms of white powder.

I will tell you.

Go and find some white powder,
white flour.
Make it into a loaf
and bring it to my table.
I will bless it and break it.
It shall be for you my body
crucified and raised.

As you eat it,
the healing of the landscape will begin,
the re-building of homes will begin,
the renewal of health will begin
because you will be the leaven
of the renewed creation.

You shall go to your work
in mining and medicine
in law-making and laboratories,
the Holy Spirit showing you
what you shall be there,
what you shall do there.

Michael Powell 1990

The bread of life

Jesus said,
'I am the bread of life'.
Another riddle?
What did he mean?

Think of bread . . .
From what is it made?
Wheat, yeast, salt, water.
Wholesome natural products,
environmentally friendly.
Living, life-giving, flavoursome, preserving,
cleansing.

How is it made?
By binding together those ingredients,
working them, taking time over them,
being patient, allowing them to be,
to create something new.

For what is it made?
For the good of the human creation
to sustain life.
The staff of life.

Jesus said,
'I am the bread of life' . . .
. . . find me in the bread of life, the ordinary,
the breakfast, the sandwiches,
the taken for granted.
I am the raw materials, the process,
the finished product, the sustainer,
the customer.

Jesus, pointing the way to God
who is in the whole of life, in you, in me.
Binding us together with love and infinite
patience for the good of all.

Kathleen Allen 1995

Endings and peace

At the ending of the day

Ever present God,
you watch unceasing
over all creation
as a mother
regards her child.
Draw near
to those
for whom we pray.
By the breath of your Spirit
     support the weak,
     restore the sick,
     comfort the sorrowful,
     console the bereaved,
     reassure the dying;
be their light
and ours
     this night
     and always,
through Jesus Christ our Lord.

Kenneth Carveley 1995

Contra-genesis

On the last day man destroyed the world called Earth.

Earth had been beautiful
until the spirit of man moved across her face
destroying all things.

And man said, 'Let there be darkness.'
Man found the darkness to be good
and called it 'Security'.
And man divided himself
into races and religions and social classes.
And there was neither dusk nor dawn
on the seventh day before all ended.

And man said, 'Let there be a strong government
to reign over our darkness.
Let there be armies so we can kill each other
with order and efficiency in the darkness;
Let us hunt and destroy those who tell the truth,
here and unto the ends of the earth,
for we like our darkness.'
And there was neither dusk nor dawn
on the sixth day before all ended.

And man said, 'Let there be rockets and bombs
so we can kill more quickly and easily.'
And there were gas chambers and ovens
to better finish the task.
It was the fifth day before all ended.

And man said, 'Let there be drugs
and other means of escape:
for there is this slight but constant irritant
– called REALITY–
that disturbs our comfort.'
It was the fourth day before all ended.

And man said, 'Let there be divisions between
      the nations
so we can know
the name of our enemy.'
It was the third day before all ended.

Finally man said,
'Let us make God in our image and likeness,
so no other God will arise to compete with us.
Let us say that God thinks as we think,
hates as we hate,
and kills as we kill.'
It was the second day before all ended.

On the last day
a great blast shook the face of the Earth;
Fire purged that beautiful terrestrial ball,
and all was silent.

And the Lord God saw
what man had done,
And in the silence
that engulfed the smoking ruins,
God wept.

Anon. 1988
(*from Nicaragua*)

On the sudden loss of a child

We left him
sleeping,
fed, washed, warm,
rested content
and loved
beyond measure . . .
but
a breath away
chance
        changed
loving to loss,
extinguished joy
in
numbed aching whyness,
bewildered wishing . . .

Kyrie eleison
Help us Lord,

till
we can leave him
sleeping,
fed, washed, warm
rested content
and loved
beyond measure . . .

Kyrie eleison
Help us Lord,

in unbelief
beyond fate
blind chance
and risk
to hope
still
You call
the children . . .

Kenneth Carveley 1989

After a still-birth

A mother's Communion preparation

Where will the tears be heard?
Where will the grief be seen?
Where will the misery be felt,
And the anguish be received?
Where is the absorption,
If there is not God?

If God is not there,
What happens to all the suffering?

It lives on,
Unheard by deafness,
Unseen by blindness,
Not perceived in cosmic emptiness.
It remains,
Unconsoled and unredeemed.

This is not the same life,
Not the same family;
It has all moved on,
Never to be the same again.
The very world divides,
Between those parents
Who have gazed upon the bodies
Of their own dead children;
And those who have not.

Words fail,
Thoughts and feelings
Lie inarticulate
In silence;
The sadness moves on,
To become silence and stillness.

For if God is not,
Then everything here is meaningless,
And worse than that,
Devalued, for everything goes by default.
The Lord is here;
His spirit is with us,
Whether it's true,
Or not –
Risk eternity on that;
Receive this body,
Receive this blood;
Receive strange gifts
Offered within the darkness.

Edwina Sherrington 1989

The source of peace: an intercession

*My dear friends, do not be bewildered by the fiery
ordeal that is upon you. (I Peter 4.12)
Their Maker will not fail them. (I Peter 4.19)*

Living Lord, in a dark hour you spoke of the gift of peace.
We seek that gift for ourselves. Grant us, we pray, the inner
serenity which you alone can give that we may become
messengers of peace to a strife-torn world.

Leader	Give peace in our time, O Lord.
People	*Give peace in our hearts, O Lord.*

We pray for all who suffer for their fidelity to the calling to be
your witnesses; all who suffer for trying to live by the truth they
have received and all who are slandered, ill-treated, falsely
imprisoned or tortured. Crucified and risen Lord, may they,
sharing your anguish, know that they will also share your
victory.

Leader	Give peace in our time, O Lord.
People	*Give peace in our hearts, O Lord.*

We pray for all who suffer as a result of the wickedness and
folly of others. We especially pray for those who suffer from
the breakdown of law and order, or from the absence of just
and humane laws and are thus denied the freedom to realise
their birthright as your children on this earth.

Leader	Give peace in our time, O Lord.
People	*Give peace in our hearts, O Lord.*

We pray for those who are fighting; injury, disfigurement,
death, their constant companions; nerves and bodies strained
beyond endurance, the streams of compassion drying up within
them, their only goal the destruction of the 'enemy'.

Whatever the colour of their skin – we pray for them.
Whatever the sound of their tongue – we pray for them.
Whatever the insignia they wear – we pray for them.

Leader   Give peace in our time, O Lord.
People   *Give peace in our hearts, O Lord.*

We pray for all who have been broken in battle; for those
who weep and for those who can no longer weep; for
those who feel the anguish and for those who have lost the
capacity to feel; for all prisoners and for all jailers; for those
who exist in war-torn lands and for those who no longer
have a homeland.

Leader   Give peace in our time, O Lord.
People   *Give peace in our hearts, O Lord.*

We pray for all who stir up strife; for all who make a profit
out of the misery of others; for all who are led into vice as
they seek a momentary forgetfulness; and for all who believe
that war is inevitable.
We bring to you particular needs . . . and we remember
those who have died.
Lord, we pray that you may hold us fast amidst all the evils
of this world that at the last we may enter into the peace and
joy of your kingdom.

Leader   Give peace in our time, O Lord.
People   *Give peace in our hearts, O Lord.*

Edmund Banyard 1991

In time of anxiety or fear

Lord, when you shared our humanity
you knew the sorrows of our race:
you sensed the clouds of a threatening future.
To our times of darkness and fear
bring the consolation and light
of your healing presence:
> *Lord, in your mercy hear our prayer*

Daphne Fraser 1993

Listen

'Listen to the voice of the Lord and enter into His peace'

Listen, to the gentle lapping of the waves
    It is the breath of God.
Listen, to the roaring of the waves
    It is the power of God.
Listen, to the shifting sands
    It is the whisper of the Lord.

Listen, to the song of the birds
    It is the praise of God.
Listen, to the rustle of the leaves
    It is the sigh of God.
Listen, to the thunder and the gale
    It is the might of the Lord.

Listen, to the music and the song
    They are the joy of God.
Listen, to the rain and the mist
    They are the tears of God.
Listen, to the sound of the snow
    It is the sympathy of the Lord.

Listen, to a baby's cry,
    a mother's sigh,
    an old man's groan,
    It is the Lord who speaks.
Listen, to those who cry for justice,
    to those who plead for peace,
    It is the Lord who speaks.

Listen, to the restlessness of your heart,
    the depth of your feelings,
    the ideas of your mind,
    It is the Lord who speaks.
Listen, to the silence,
    to the noise,
    It is the Lord who speaks.

Answer him.

Anne Doyle 1996

For mourners

Let us pray for those who mourn:

God, loving N . . .
nearer to us than our next breath

Be with those who mourn.
Be in their shock, their grief
their anger and despair
that they may grieve
but not as those without hope.

Forgive all the harm they (we) feel
they have done to N . . . and
show them that they are forgiven.

We offer to you
all the regrets
the memories
the pain
the 'if onlys'
knowing that you
will surround those we mourn
with your presence
and heal them and us
and all that harms us.

Kate McIlhagga 1988

Peace be with you

John 20.19-23

Shame-faced, once the first shock subsided.
Seeing the dead alive is a joyous thing –
but what of his last glimpse of us –
showing a clean pair of heels
in his time of need!

Much-needed, that greeting,
'Peace be with you.'
Peace spreading wide, sinking deep,
as he shows his hands and side.

'Forgive.'
Do not blame
yourself or others for the past.
If you retain those wrongs
they'll still exist to mar the world.

'Receive the Holy Spirit.'
Open up to peace.

Hilda Mary r.a. 1991

Standing on the edge

Leaving,
bidding goodbye,
away from the familiar,
the known, the loved,
alone, yet not . . .
looking beyond to the distant hope.
The wastes of death encroach,
clustered, poised,
ready to strike,
to engulf.
Yet in the engulfing waves
glory beckons.
Fear and peace stand
shoulder to shoulder,
as certainty and insecurity
vie with each other.

Is love decaying,
or is it truly being made whole?
Are the clouds of gloom
really images of the presence of God?
Love has held me fast,
love holds me now,
does love lead me on?
Life ends,
grief, tears, parting;
my cross awaits . . .
Beyond –
my Easter Day.

G. M. Breffitt 1991

God's peace

From Nigeria – originally a hymn in the Igbo language

There is nothing that man desires so much
  as God's peace.
This world's wealth does not bring such
  happiness
  as the peace of God.

> *True peace,*
> *that's the secret of happiness.*
> *The turmoil of the world, the shocks of*
>   *the world,*
> *are calmed in the abiding presence*
> *of that peace of God.*

The wisdom of the world
  cannot compare with God's peace.
The honours of the world
  can never be like God's peace.

Power and victory will not lead you
  to God's peace.
Tricks and treachery will never procure you
  God's peace.

I long with all my heart to have around me
  God's peace.
What must I do to receive in my heart this gift
  of God's peace?

Prayer alone will help you to partake
  of God's peace.
For it is Jesus, and Jesus alone, who will
  bring you
  God's peace.

Ikoli Harcourt Whyte 1988
(Translated by the Very Revd Ebere O. Nze)

Blessings and benedictions

Nothing can separate us from the love of God,
>We go in faith to live as the people of God.

And may God who is the beginning
be with you in your new life.
God who is at the centre
be your meaning and purpose.
And God who calls us forward
travel with you beyond the known path.

May our feet follow the footsteps of God this day.
>O God, may we do your will this day.

May our mouths praise the love of God this day.
>O God, may we do your will this day.

May our ears hear the words of God and obey them.
>O God, may we do your will this day.

>>>>*(from Japan)*

May the God who shakes heaven and earth,
whom death could not contain,
who lives to disturb and heal us,
bless you with power to go forth
and proclaim the gospel.

>>>*Janet Morley*
>>*(Reproduced from* All Desires Known, *SPCK, 1992)*

May the love of the cross,
the power of the resurrection
and the presence of the Living Lord
be with you always.
And the blessing of the Eternal God,
Creator and Sustainer,
Risen Lord and Saviour,
Giver of holiness and love,
be upon you now and evermore.

>>>*(from Jerusalem)*

Jesus invites us to a way of celebration,
meeting and feasting with the humble and poor.
Let us walk his way with joy.

Jesus beckons us to a way of risk,
letting go of our security.
Let us walk his way with joy.

Jesus challenges us to listen to the voices
of those who have nothing to lose.
Let us walk his way with joy.

Jesus points us to a way of self-giving,
where power and status are overturned.
Let us walk his way with joy.

Jesus calls us to follow the way of the cross,
where despair is transformed
by the promise of new life.
Let us walk his way with joy.

Jan Berry 1989

At a time of death

God of the great wind
blow away death
leave with us life:
>   the life that has been,
>   the life that now is
>   in heaven and on earth,
>   the life that will be
>   for ever and ever.

God of the mighty sea
wash away grief
leave with us joy:
>   the joy that has been,
>   the joy that now is
>   in heaven and on earth,
>   the joy that will be
>   for ever and ever.

God of the brilliant sun
burn away pain
leave with us power:
>   the power that has been,
>   the power that now is
>   in heaven and on earth,
>   the power that will be
>   for ever and ever.

Michael Powell 1989

Prayers for everyday life

We belong to one another

Jesus Christ
who reached across
the ethnic boundaries between
Samaritan, Roman,
Syro-Phoenician and Jew,
who offered fresh sight
to the blind
and freedom to the captives,
help us to break down the barriers
in our community,
enable us to see the reality
of racism and bigotry
and free us to challenge
and uproot them –
from ourselves, our society
and our world.

Churches' Commission for Racial Justice 1996

Aching void

Tonight Lord, I ache inside
I ache for the not-so-very-old woman told
    she has only a few weeks to live
I ache for her courage and her determination
    to fight to the end
I offer the comfort of communion but . . .
'No . . . not yet . . . I will get to church and
    kneel once more at His Table,' she smiled.

Her breath rasped. The hole gapes where
    the tube has been removed and she has to
    cover with fluttering fingers to speak . . .
    She watches my eyes . . . 'I just ask God to
    close it,' she said, 'and it is getting smaller!'

I ache for her smile
I ache for her as she hopes to see her new
    grand-daughter
And I remember . . .
I remember that it is only a few months since
    another young mother faced chemotherapy
    with trepidation.
I remember how I ached for her bewildered
    young family in their sorrow and anguish.
And I remember her radiant smile last week
    at the news of no further traces as we praised
    You together, Lord.
And I remember . . .
I remember my own unshed tears
And the ache that never quite heals in spite of
    the passing of many years
And I wonder, Lord . . .
I wonder how You coped with the sorrow of
    others as You bore such sorrow in Yourself.
Lord, I offer you my aching emptiness.
Fill the void with Your love yet once more,
    that I might be used to minister through the
    ache to others.

Mary Teed 1992

Mr Ordinary

Lord, I feel ever so ordinary.

I'm an ordinary sort of friend.
I'll borrow my mate's spanner . . . and forget to give it back.

I'm an ordinary sort of dad.
I love my kids but . . .
. . . but sometimes I'm just too tired.
On goes the tele . . .

I'm an ordinary sort of husband.
But I expect,
and I use.

I'm not a bad chap, I suppose.
I stayed with Dave when he had his breakdown.
I love to let the kids jump in puddles . . .
I make Irish potato bread for the wife,
Saturday nights . . .

I'm an ordinary sort of bloke
you know, Lord,
Mr Average – not especially good at anything;
okay at most things.

Bent nose, nice smile, balding –
Average sort of chap.
Nothing outstanding about me.
Sort of Mr Average. Mr Ordinary.

Well, Bless Me
And I thought you were quite extraordinary
Said the Lord.

Jonathan Martin 1991

Technology

Creator God,
there are many faces to the world
you bring into being
day by day, moment by moment.
One face is the face of things,
things that work and move,
things that do things,
things that used well, enrich life,
the technological face.

You bring into being
the world of technology
and entrust it to us,
to develop it,
to manage it,
to give it meaning and value.

We thank you for the technology
that enriches the life of the home and the
        shops, of the office, the factory
        and the site.
We thank you for the technology
that is part of medicine and healing,
        that is part of science and exploration.

But, Lord, the downside,
        the technology of warfare,
                the technology of manipulation,
                        the technology that destroys natural places,
the technology that destroys human
        communities pointlessly.
Yours, and ours if we are close to you, is the pain
        of seeing good things used for bad ends.

Lord, despite your pain, you do not go back
        on your decision to entrust
                choice and decision and judgement
                to us.

So we pray for all technologists and engineers,
    all designers and makers of things,
        in every field of human endeavour,
            that they may judge well what
            they do.

Open to us all the mystery
    of yourself, ever-creating God,
        and ourselves, your trusted people,
          one, together,
            in the world of good things,
            good technology.

We ask these prayers
    in the name of Jesus,
        maker of things, and Christ.

Michael Powell 1991

Windows

O God our Father, we give you thanks for your ever-loving
concern for all your people, in all their activities.

We thank you that you are always ready to meet and talk
with your people and draw them and their tasks into your
way and your purposes.

We pray for all people who make and fit and paint and
clean the windows of the world's buildings.

We pray for all who design and create the displays in
shop windows.

We pray for all artists in stained glass that they may see
and share true visions.

We remember Daniel who opened his window towards
Jerusalem that his prayers might flow out over the World.
Today, we let our prayers flow out to Jerusalem itself, to the
Middle East and to all places where peace is, at best, fragile.

We reflect on death, a window between this world and the
next, praising you that in the death and resurrection of Jesus
it is a clear and open window.

We pray for the Church, that in all her communions
she may be a clear window by which the world
may see into your very heart.

In Christ's name.

Michael Powell 1991

A story of God's heart

Creative heart

'In the beginning . . . God created.' (*Genesis 1.1*)
Heart breathing. . .
    pulsating with love
        penetrating through darkness
            overflowing like a river
                erupting earth
            creating life
        imaging Self
    resting with contentment
'God looked at everything he had made,
    and he found it very good.' (*Genesis 1.31*)

Wounded heart

'Woe is me! I am undone,
my wound is incurable.' (*Jeremiah 10.19*)
Heart grieving . . .
    yearning for the beloved
        desolating pain
            weeping fountains of tears
                anguishing anger
            waiting with weariness
        mourning in darkness
    longing for union
'I call you back
    like a wife forsaken and grieved in spirit,
    a wife married in youth and then cast off.' (*Isaiah 54.6*)

Pursuing heart

'How can I give you up, O Ephraim!
How shall I surrender you, O Israel.' (*Hosea 11.8*)
Heart espousing . . .
    searching eagerly
      seeking with passion
        promising a land overflowing
          drawing with bands of love
        alluring to a desert
      speaking tenderly
    ravishing with love
'I will espouse you to me forever;
I will espouse you in right and justice
    in love and in mercy;
I will espouse you in fidelity,
    and you shall know the Lord.' (*Hosea 2.19-20*)

Enfleshed heart

'In the beginning was the Word;
the Word was in God's presence
and the Word was God.' (*John 1:1*)
Heart conceiving . . .
    filling-full the promise
      overshadowing with love
        erupting into human life
          leaping with joy
        waiting in stillness
      springing forth from a womb
    birthing light into darkness
'The Word became flesh
and made his dwelling among us.' (*John 1.14*)

Healing heart

'I have come that you may have
life, and have it to the full.' *(John 3.16)*
Heart touching . . .
   stretching out a hand
      inviting into the kingdom feast
         speaking the word of life
            enabling the blind to see
         enlivening dead bodies and broken spirits
      changing stony hearts into flesh
   reaping a harvest of life
'From within me rivers of living water shall flow
Whoever drinks the water I give
   will never be thirsty;
The water I give shall become a fountain within
   leaping up to provide life.' *(John 7.38)*

Aching heart

'How often I have yearned to gather you,
as a mother bird gathers her young
under her wings, but you refused me.' *(Matthew 23.37)*
Heart weeping . . .
   pleading with no response
      languishing unrelentlessly in love
         yearning to water dry land
            longing to enflesh hearts of stone
         hurting from rejecting hearts
      drowning in tears of vulnerability
'This people pay me lip service
but their heart is far from me.
Empty is the reverence they do me
   because they teach as dogmas
     mere human precepts.' *(Mark 7.6-7)*

Breaking heart

'My heart is filled with sorrow
to the point of death.' (*Mark 14.34*)
Heart agonizing . . .
   anguishing in inconsolable agony
     sweating drops of blood in torment
       falling to the ground to be lifted up
         stripping body of life to bring healing
         bleeding to death to pour life into death
       crying aloud in total surrender
'It is finished.' (*John 19:30*)

Burning heart

'Were not our hearts burning within us?' (*Luke 24.32*)
Heart energizing . . .
   overcoming death with new life
     entering exultantly into glory
       driving a forceful wind of fire
         pouring the flaming Spirit on the earth
       filling overflowingly with the Holy Spirit
     encouraging all to grow in communion
   challenging nations to live in peace
'Stir into flame the gift of God bestowed . . .
The Spirit God has given us is no cowardly
   Spirit, but rather one that makes
     us strong, loving, and wise.' (*2 Timothy 1.6-7*)

Maureen Conroy R.S.M. 1987

Deliver me from nice people!

Lord, I'm afraid I'm bothering you again,
wanting help over this prayer business.
My trouble this time isn't the usual afflictions
one expects to endure,
from difficult or angry people;
it's that I find it so hard to pray for
the people who are really so nice!
They're kind and sweet and they smile
forgivingly,
they are good Christians and very patient with me.
Their reactions are always the right ones;
and I want to stick pins in them.
Lord, why is it nice people
make me feel so murderous?
and why does being good
make some folk a real pain in the neck?
Deliver me from nice people, O Lord,
at least some of the time,
while I recover my strength
to encounter another set of them.
Amen

Daphne Fraser 1987

Proverbs 31 – a meditation

*A truly capable woman – who can find her? She is beyond
the price of pearls –*
Oh God, in whose eyes we are all of infinite worth, we pray
for those women who are counted as cheap labour, for low
paid women and unpaid women and for women whose work
is counted as worthless.

Give her a share in what her hands have worked for –
We pray for the women whose labour is stolen from them, for
exploited and oppressed women. We pray for justice at work,
for justice in access to work and for just rewards for work.

*She sets her mind on a field – she buys it; with what her hands
have earned she plants a vineyard –*
We pray for those women who work on the land, remembering
especially the landless peasant women who grow food that
they will never eat and harvest crops that they cannot share
with their children.

*She holds out her hands to the poor, she opens her arms to
the needy –*
We pray for those women who work for justice and peace.
For all those women who strive to end poverty, who labour
to eliminate hunger and who toil to build a lasting peace.

*She keeps good watch on the conduct of her household . . .
her children stand up and proclaim her blessed –*
We pray for those women for whom their children are their
work, for the innumerable company of women who labour
creating, nurturing and sustaining your children – the very
work of life itself – and yet receive no pay. We pray for all
women who feel undervalued, or valuelesss.

*She knows that her affairs are going well, her lamp does not
go out at night –*
We pray for women employed in business, in administration.
We give thanks for the trail-blazing women who have fought
to do work denied to them on the grounds of their sex. For
women doctors, judges, lawyers, politicians and professors.

She sets her hands to the distaff, her fingers grasp the spindle –
We pray for those women employed in the textile industry. For
those who work long hours for low wages in sweat shops, for
those whose jobs are insecure, who do not have the protection
of a strong and vigorous union.

She gets up while it is still dark giving her household their food –
We pray for those women whose work it is to provide food
that we may eat. For mothers struggling to feed their children,
for women who process food they cannot afford to buy. For
countless women working in countless cafes and restaurants,
canteens and hotels whose work goes unseen and
unrecognised.

*She puts her back into her work and shows how strong her
arms can be –*
We remember before God that in many parts of the world it is
women who perform the manual work – who build the houses
and dig the wells, who lay the roads and collect the fuel. We
pray for all women whose work requires strength and stamina
– for all whose work leaves them physically exhausted – for
those who have to work too hard.

*When she opens her mouth, she does so wisely – on her
tongue is kindly instruction –*
We pray for women whose work is that of teaching. We give
thanks for the women from whom we have learnt and for those
who have been an example to us. Especially we pray for the
women who teach our faith, for all women priests and pastors,
for women religious, for prophetesses, evangelists and
theologians.

*She is clothed in strength and dignity, she can laugh at the day
to come –*
We give thanks for the work of women, we ask you to bless it,
to clothe it with your strength and dignity. Bless this day, and
the work we shall do in it and may we laugh at the day to come.

Clare Sealy 1988

Love

It doesn't matter that I talk like a poet or sing like an angel;
if I'm no good at loving, my life is an empty thing,
all noise, no music.
It doesn't matter that I know all about religion and have faith
to work miracles;
without love, it gets me nowhere.
Or suppose I share all the firm's profits with my employees,
and then give away my share to the Third World,
or even die for a good cause –
if I act without love, I might as well not bother.

Love means being patient with people, and kind to them,
and not envying them.
It means not boasting at them,
and not being rude to them.
It means not being selfish, and not being touchy;
Love doesn't keep count of someone else's faults,
or enjoy catching them out;
it prefers to see the best in them.
Love goes on trusting, goes on hoping,
and goes on putting up with things.

Love goes on.
When a prophecy comes true, it's done with;
you don't need it any more.
When a promise is fulfilled, you don't need it any more;
you have the fulfilment.
When children grow up, they don't need toys any more;
they have the real thing.
And some day, somewhere – in heaven perhaps,
we shall have the real thing
which all our human science and art and religion
were pointing to, and then we shan't need them any more.
But there will never be a time or a place
at which people don't need love any more.

Love lasts. Well there are three things that last:
faith, and hope, and love.
But love lasts longest.

Jamie Wallace 1988

The secular is sacred

The Lord Jesus Christ
calls you to his table,
calls you by your name,
just by your name;
whether you hold
a high position in the world,
or a lowly one,
or none.

He says to us all:
bring with you your concern
for the millions in need,
for the young unemployed,
for the older unemployed.
He says: bring with you
your concern
for those caught in changes
over which they have no control;
bring with you
your concern
for the future
of your land.

He says:
do not be afraid
to talk at my table
of these things;
for your world
is the world
the Father called me to love,
the world for which
I give my life,
the world which
in the Father's time
shall share my
resurrection.

Michael Powell 1988

The gift of children

Children are:
    small lives but
    big responsibilities;
    small bodies but
    big demands.

Let us pray for all homes:
    That they may be places of love
    That they may be places of acceptance
    That they may be places of forgiveness
    That they may be places where
    both adults and children can grow
    That they may be places where
    we can be ourselves.

Let us pray for all parents:
    That they may create loving, caring homes
    That they may treat their children as persons
    That they may accept that there is no such thing
    as a perfect parent or a perfect child
    That they may not be overwhelmed with guilt
    That they may have joy in their children

Let us pray for all children:
    That they might have a happy and secure childhood
    That they might not be warped or spoilt in any way
    That they might learn to cope with themselves and with others
    That they might grow up to be loving and caring adults

    Small lives but
    big responsibilities
    Small bodies but
    big demands.

Help us, Lord, to work together and with you in home, church
and community to make the society we have prayed for become
a living reality, part of your kingdom whose rule is love.
                    Amen.

Christine Odell 1988

A prayer for unity and peace

As we ask that our prayers may be answered by God,
so may we be ready to respond to the call of the Holy Spirit.

May our spiritual pilgrimage lead our feet into the way
of peace.

Let us not despair in the times of darkness,
nor be blinded by the light which illuminates our path,
but go forward trusting our way will become clear.

May we rejoice in the high places and be sustained in
the depths.

Help us to listen to our families and friends,
    to our neighbours,
    both oppressed and free,
    and to those of other countries
    and other faiths,
that we may be reconciled with them,
for each has his or her story of experiences
on the path to that Truth which passes all understanding.

From a group of Friends (Quakers) meeting
for a family weekend at Hengrave Hall 1992

For times of relaxation

Life-fulfilling God,
we thank you for the joy
of belonging to you and to each other.
Help us who seek to serve,
to learn also how to relax,
how to have fun, how to let go of our fixed images,
that together we may discover new experiences:
the adventure of games;
the healing release of laughter;
the togetherness of sharing fun;
the common sense in sometimes doing silly things;
the wealth of giving more than we can receive;
the humility of receiving more than we can give.
God of laughter, God of fun, God of exuberance
help us dare to remove the masks behind which we hide,
that we may be ourselves in company with your people.

David Blanchflower 1992

Tapestry

The Weaver builds a loom
With time and space
For warp and weft.
She chooses colours and material.
Now we, Her living threads,
Must make the picture.

W.S. Beattie 1992

Meditation with silence

In stillness
And silence
I know
You are my God
And I love you

Period of silence

There is no
Felt awareness
But deeper inside
Than I knew existed
I am with you

Period of silence

All else
Is of no account
My pride, self-doubt
Inhibitions
Washed aside

Period of silence

Held in being
Loved into life
Delicately balanced
Joy transcending
Aching anguish

Period of silence

Called by name
Compelled by love
Desiring nothing
Except your will
Expressed in me

Christine Bull 1992

An old person prays

Dear Father God, we come to you
in earnest supplication;
we want to serve you to the end
but lack the dedication

to battle through the many trials
our ageing bodies give us,
and need your strength to overcome
the failures ever with us.

Our memories are faltering,
our knees will hardly bear
the weight we put upon them
when we try to climb a stair;

when we crave the fire and armchair
when we should be craving you
and know that we're the losers
when your will we fail to do.

Be patient Lord – we stumble on,
we know that you are near,
have heard our prayers, will answer us –
pray grant the words we hear

be, 'Well done, good and faithful servant!
Come, the way is clear,
Heaven has opened wide her doorway,
enter without fear.'

Lillian Columbine 1990

Out of the depths

That prayer about offering myself
To be a living sacrifice –
I said the words each time, and thought
I meant them. But I didn't think you'd
Take them quite so seriously! Is this
What it means, to be put down.
Over and over again? It
Hardly seems worth making the effort
To offer ideas, or even to do my best
In the work you have given me to do.
And the people I struggle to love –
I suppose it was you who
Gave them to me, Lord? I wasn't
Wrong about that as well?

Strange how you kept reminding me
That you were there.
In the power of the Spirit -
I said those words each time,
And didn't take them seriously.
Time after time, when I'd been
Chewed up and spat out, you came
With life and courage, hope and
Saving humour. I know you never said
It would be easy, but Lord,
Did it have to be that hard?

And then, life and work, arena and
Agenda, mysteriously transformed.
It takes me by surprise
Each time it happens, and my heart
Sings to your praise and glory.

Ann Lewin 1989

Free to be

No matter who I am
Or where I've been
No matter what I've done
Or what I've seen

No matter what I have
Or where I go
No matter what I do
Or how I grow

No matter what I risk
Or what I fear
No matter what I face
Or what is near

No matter what the days
Or what the years
No matter what my joys
Or all my tears

God will direct me
God will correct me
God will protect me

God will accept me.

John Stuart 1989

It is not uncommon to talk to God

A poem written from prison on Robben Island

Particularly in a single cell,
but even in the sections
the religious sense asserts itself;

perhaps a childhood habit of nightly prayers
the accessibility of Bibles,
or awareness of the proximity of death;

and of course, it is a currency –
pietistic expressions can purchase favours
and it is a way of suggesting reformation
(which can procure promotion);

and the resort of the weak
is to invoke divine revenge
against a rampaging injustice;

but in the grey silence of the empty afternoons
it is not uncommon
to find oneself talking to God.

Dennis Brutus 1989

Sleepless nights

I sit alone in my room.
All the world sleeps except for me
and the distant air of a radio
crooning ceaselessly into the
midnight air.

Is it a radio I hear, Lord,
or the voices of your angels,
pronouncing benediction on the
world as humankind sleeps unaware
of your eternal vigil?

'All you need is love',
the refrain rings clear, but
is that really all you need?
Love doesn't pay the rent;
love doesn't feed the kids;
love doesn't help me sleep in a
world that lies blissfully unaware
of my pain, my problems, my heartache.

Now the radio-angels' voices have faded.
Perhaps even radio-angels need to sleep!
Now I am alone, totally alone,
unsleeping, unresting, unhappy.
Will no one watch with me through the
darkness of the long, lonely night?

My child, I was alone that night in Gethsemane.
I was afraid, pained, lonely.
No radio-angels spoke to me of love,
though love was my destiny.
I waited knowing yet unknowing,
hoping against hope,
drinking deep from the cup of
loneliness in which you share.

All you need is love,
my love,
to help you face the darkness of
these darkest moments,
and emerge triumphant into
the glorious radiance of a new day.

G. M. Breffitt 1989

Meditation on the Lord's Prayer

From Central America

Our Father
who is in those who suffer because
they have no bread;
who is in those who go out
and don't come back,
in the tortured and the murdered.
Our Father,
who is in us here on earth.

Holy is your name
in the stars
which dance in children's eyes;
in the hungry who share their bread;
in the strength of those who,
insulted and beaten,
give themselves so that love,
land and life
can be for everyone.

Your kingdom come
Your kingdom,
which is a generous land
which flows with milk and honey;
a shared land,
where confidence and truth reign,
where life flourishes
in all its fullness.

Let us do your will
standing up when others sit;
raising our voice when all are silent;
accepting ill treatment, yet
sowing confidence in the soil of fear
and cultivating
the flower of understanding
and the tree of hope.

You are giving us our daily bread
in the song of the bird
and the miracle of the corn,
in the strength of our hands
united to fight for life;
in the return of land
or a fairer wage;
and in the comfort
of the hand stretched out
to relieve our pain.

Forgive us
when we hurt a beloved friend;
when we keep silent
in the face of injustice;
when we bury our dreams;
and when we fail to share
bread, wine, love and land.

Don't let us fall into the temptation
of shutting the door through fear;
of resigning ourselves
to hunger and injustice;
of taking up the same weapons
as the enemy is using
or of thinking that a more just society
is already your kingdom.

But deliver us from the evil
of intrigues and mistrust
which arise to break
the loving ties which unite us;
give us the perseverance
to tread the path of love
even if we fall and hurt
a brother or sister,

or spike ourselves with thorns;
even though we die:
we shall have known
your kingdom
which is for ever and ever.

Author unknown 1990

Index of authors

Ainger, Geoffrey   117
Allen, Kathleen   155
Anon.   25, 147, 159
Author unknown   140, 201

Bailey, Simon   59
Banyard, Edmund   23, 54, 148, 164
Beattie, W. S.   193
Berry, Jan   173
Blackledge, Denis   14, 21, 35
Blanchflower, David   49, 76, 145, 193
Breffitt, G. M.   50, 170, 199
Brice, Peter   125
Brutus, Dennis   198
Bull, Christine   194

Carveley, Kenneth   37, 38, 97, 112, 158, 158
Cashmore, Gwen and Puls, Joan   12
Churches' Commission for Racial Justice   176
Columbine, Lillian   195
Conroy, Maureen R. S. M.   182
Crawshaw, Margaret   91
Creed, Denise   139
Cross, Hugh   108

Day, Peggy   90
Doyle, Anne   167
Dykes, Alastair   118

Fageol, Suzanne   99
Flynn, David   92
Ford, David J.   56
Fraser, Daphne   115, 130, 152, 166, 186
Friends' meeting, Hengrave Hall   192

Gilbert, Vince   18, 31
Gumley House School pupils   128

Hamilton, Roddy   82, 88
Hares, Betty   135

Hilda Mary   52, 169

Jackson, Brenda   94, 138
Jenkins, Davidv74, 105
Jenkins, Stuart   114
Jones, Christine   29

Lathrop, Chuck   78
Lewin, Ann   2, 5, 40, 46, 50, 196

McIlhagga, Kate   4, 69, 120, 122, 168
Martin, Jonathan   123, 178
Morley, Janet   10, 80, 172

Newman, Adrian   72
Nitobe, Inazo   151

Odell, Christine   6, 191
Oldershaw, John   8
Owen, David M.   96

Powell, Michael   48, 149, 154, 174, 179, 181, 190
Puls, Joan and Cashmore, Gwen   12

Rackley, John   102
Ratcliff, Eva   47
Reid, Ron   70
Rust, Godfrey   121, 124

St James' Church, New York   131
Sealy, Clare   187
Sherrington, Edwina   58, 162
Slee, Nicola   133
Smart, Ernest   67
Smith, Allan R.   106
Smith-Cameron, Ivor   85
Steel, Lesley   0
Stevens, Judith   16
Stevens, Sheelah   75
Stokes, Adrian   43
Stuart, John   197

Teed, Mary   132, 177
Temple, David   17
Thompson, Bruce D.   24, 25
Thorogood, Bernard   7

Wakelin, Rosemary   42
Walder, Morag   142

Wallace, Jamie   3, 189
Wangusa, Helen   28
Weifan, Wang   41
Weoley Castle Community Church
   141
Whyte, Ikoli Harcourt   171
Wilson, Duncan   9

Index of titles

Aching void   177
Affirmation of faith   88
After Christmas   50
After a still-birth   162
Agriculture and rural life   149
Angels   40
Annunciation   37
Ash Wednesday   52
Aspiration   3
At the ending of the day   158
At a time of death   174
Authority from being sufferers with
   Christ   123

Be still   2
Become our resurrection   105
Before the Easter icon   97
Before the harvest   148
Being still   24
Belonging: children's meditations and
   prayers   128
Blessings and benedictions   172
Bone of my Bone   10
Bread of life   155
Bus to Emmaus   94
But nobody went to his burial   102

Call to worship   31
Carol for a dark age   42
Child's prayer at the crib   47
Christ the healer   108
Christmas   49
Christmas Communion   48
Come Emmanuel   29
Come as a girl   28
Contra-genesis   159
Creator God   9
Credo from Nicaragua   147
Cross-carrying Jesus: a prayer of
   confession   69

Dancer   141
Dandelion   139
Deliver me from nice people!   186
Disciple   121

Disclosure   5
Dying stranger   74

Easter prayer   92

For mourners   168
For times of relaxation   193
Free to be   197

Gardener   91
Gift of children   191
God's peace   171
Good Friday   58

Hanta Yo   12
He came to his own home   41
Healing of laughter   132
Heard at Harvest   138
Help us to admit our emptiness   122
Help us to be true to our calling   145
Holy Saturday   76
Holy Spirit come   117

I ask for daily bread   151
In search of a roundtable   78
In time of anxiety or fear   166
Incarnation   46
It is not uncommon to talk to God
   198

Laodicean estate agent writes   124
Listen   167
Listening in   14
Litany of thanksgiving   112
Lord of life – feed me   25
Love   189
Love, truth and openness   118

Magnificat: the mystery of Mary   38
Meditation – nails   72
Meditation on the Lord's Prayer   201
Meditation with silence   194
Meditation on a storm   115
Morning   8
Mr Ordinary   178

index of titles

Nine seasonal collects 99

An old person prays 195
On the edge 125
On entering church 16
On the sudden loss of a child 161
Out of the depths 196

Palm Sunday 54
Peace be with you 169
Powerful silence 75
Prayer of confession 17
Prayer for the parish 131
Prayer of preparation 6
Prayer rosary 120
Prayer for unity and peace 192
Prayers of adoration and confession
  18
Proverbs 31 – a meditation 187
Psalm of Falling and Rising 106

Question of language 130

Reflection 85
Resurrection 90
Round the back in Bethlehem 43

Secular is sacred 190
Send your Holy Spirit 133
Seven days 7
Sleepless nights 199

So many things I can't believe 23
Source of peace, an intercession 164
Standing on the edge 170
Still waiting 35
Stones cry out . . . 67
Story of God's heart 182
Supper 82

Tapestry 193
Tears 56
Technology 179
Thank you for your presence with us
  135
This is the day they call good 70
This is my . . . 96
Three farmers 142
Tingle factor 21
To women and to men 80
Twelfth Night 50

Way 30
We belong to one another 176
Web of creation 152
White powder 154
Who travelled to follow Christ's Way
  114
Why I never wash . . . 25
Windows 181
Women and the Cross 59
Word awaited 4
Work is love made visible 140

Index of first lines

A Christian must be like a dancer 141
A truly capable woman 187
Across the ages ring two cries 54
As we ask that our prayers may be answered by God 192
As you stagger on your lonely journey 69

Be, do not do 6
Be gentle when you touch bread 85
Before the harvest 148
Bread and Wine 82
Break forth into shouts of joy 31
Bright moon, scattered stars 41

Children are 191
Christ our friend 101
Christ our true Mother 101
Come Emmanuel 29
Concerning the why and how and what 78
Creator God, taking undiluted delight 9
Creator God, there are many faces to the world 179

Dear Father God, we come to you 195
Dear God thank you for your presence with us 135
Dear Lord, shepherds came to you 47
Did He who sent the messenger 37
Disturb us, Lord, when we are too well 131
Dying Stranger your arms stretch wide 74

Ever present God 158

Flames of Fire, shafts of illumination 40

God above 28
God challenge and awaken us 42
God of the Falling and of the Rising 106

God of the great wind 174
God of surprises 12
God of terror and joy 99
God, why is it so much of our Christianity 130
Good Friday and they had it right 58

He had let the rest down 102
Her face was turned from me 91
He's grown, that Baby 46
Hiroshima 120
Holy Child of Bethlehem 49
Holy Spirit come 117

I am the Way 30
I am the woman who anointed Jesus 59
I ask for daily bread 151
I believe in God, creator of an unfinished world 147
I live in a world 152
I saw the pain in your faces 154
I sit alone in my room 199
I was made to wash as a child 25
I will follow you 121
I'd never heard a real 'rushing mighty wind' 115
Imagining 7
In the beginning, a garden 90
'In the beginning . . . God created' 182
In stillness 194
It doesn't matter that I talk like a poet or sing like an angel 189
It is morning . . . 8
It looks much as it did before 50

Jesus Christ who reached across 176
Jesus invites us to a way of celebration 173
Jesus said, 'I am the bread of life' 155
Jesus the stones cry out 67

Keep in mind that you are dust 52

Lady, caught in swift surprise 38

Leaving, bidding goodbye   170
Let us picture the farms of East Anglia   149
Let us pray for those who have authority   123
Let us pray for those who mourn   168
Life-fulfilling God   193
Like a dandelion, my faith grows   139
Listen, to the gentle lapping of the waves   167
Living on the edge of the church   125
Living God save us   105
Living Lord, in a dark hour   164
Living Lord, send your Holy Spirit   133
Lord, I feel ever so ordinary   178
Lord, I'm afraid I'm bothering you again   186
Lord Jesus Christ, who enduredLord, I'm afraid I'm bothering you again   186
Lord Jesus Christ, who enduredLord, I'm afraid I'm bothering you again   186
Lord Jesus Christ, who endured   108
Lord of life – feed me this day   25
Lord of life, you shared our life   56
Lord, we thank you that you have called us   145
Lord, when you shared our humanity   166
Lord, your house seems noisy   16
Loving Creator, we confess that as women   10
Loving Lord, we are still waiting   35
Loving Lord, you are the one who is always there for me   14
Loving Lord, you invite and excite me   21

Matthias the innkeeper had had a rotten day   43
May the God who shakes heaven and earth   172
May the love of the cross   172
May the risen Christ who called Mary by her name   92
My name is Meliakim   72

No matter who I am   197
Nothing can separate us from the love

of God   172

O Eternal Wisdom   80
O God our deliverer   102
O God our Father, we give you thanks   181
O God for whom we long   101
O God whose greeting we miss   100
O God, you call us to commitment   101
O God, you withdraw from our sight   102
On the last day man destroyed the world called Earth   159
One year three farmers prepared their land   142
Our Father who is in those who suffer   201

Particularly in a single cell   198
Prayer is like watching for the kingfisher   5

Rejection is what I face   128
Remember them   112
Rise up! Lord of the Living   97
Risen Christ   100

Shame-faced, once the first shock subsided   169
Sometimes   4
Sorry, I didn't see you standing there   94
Spirit hovering over our chaos   122

Teach me to laugh, Lord   132
That prayer about offering myself   196
That we may learn   3
The developers have moved in   124
The Lord Jesus Christ calls you to his table   190
'The nights are closing in'   138
The stable is empty now   50
The Weaver builds a loom   193
There are so many things I can't believe   23
There are things   118
There is nothing that man desires so much   171
They whipped Him   75

This is the day they call good   70
This is my Body   96
This table is our Bethlehem   48
Today we have stood at the morning
    of the kingdom   88
Tonight Lord, I ache inside   177

Wait, my friends, it is not over yet   76
We come from a busy world   24
We left him sleeping   161

We praise you, God   114
We're all different, Lord   17
Where will the tears be heard?   162
Why are you waiting, people of the
    living God?   18
Work is love made visible   140

You do not have to look for anything
    2

Acknowledgements

The publisher gratefully acknowledges permission to reproduce copyright material in this publication. The copyright of the items included belongs in each case to the individuals who wrote them. Every effort has been made to trace and contact these copyright holders. If there are inadvertent omissions we apologize to those concerned and will ensure that a suitable acknowledgement is made at the next reprint.

The collected material may be read or reproduced in the context of worship services or similar events but other use or reproduction requires specific consent, which should be sought in the first instance from Churches Together in Britain and Ireland.

Scripture quotation (**10**) from *The Revised Standard Version of the Bible* is copyright © 1946, 1952 and 1971 by the Division of Christian Education of the National Council of Churches in the USA. Used by permission. All rights reserved.

Scripture quotation (**29**) from *Revised English Bible* © Oxford University Press and Cambridge University Press 1989.

Janet Morley, 'To women and to men' (**80–81**) and 'Blessing and benedictions' (**172**) from *All Desires Known*, SPCK 1992.

Godfrey Rust, 'A Laodicean estate agent writes' (**124**) from 'Welcome to the real world', *Collected Poems and Performance Pieces 1980 – 2000*, Wordsout Publications, www.wordsout.co.uk